Great American Dream Machines

Great American
CLASSIC CARS
Jay Hirsch

Dream Machines
OF THE 50s AND 60s

Macmillan Publishing Company   NEW YORK
Collier Macmillan Publishers   LONDON

Macmillan Publishing Company
866 Third Avenue, New York, N.Y. 10022
Collier Macmillan Canada, Inc.

Library of Congress Cataloging-in-Publication Data

Hirsch, Jay.
　Great American dream machines.

　Includes index.
　1. Automobiles—United States. I. Title.
TL23.H56　1985　　629.2′222′0973　　85-10454
ISBN 0-02-551830-5

Macmillan books are available at special discounts for bulk purchases for sales promotions, premiums, fund-raising, or educational use. For details, contact:
　Special Sales Director
　Macmillan Publishing Company
　866 Third Avenue
　New York, N.Y. 10022

10 9 8 7 6 5 4 3 2 1

MANUFACTURED IN ITALY BY MONDADORI
Design by Antler & Baldwin, Inc.

Contents

Contents

Introduction

How do you define a dream machine? Who sets the standard? Without trying to get too confusing there will be two definitions. One is for this book, and one is for and from Detroit

A dream machine is a fantasy or "dream" car that lives in an individual's mind. Many cars fall into this group, owing to their popularity and collectibility. The 2-seat T-Birds and the later 4-seater or "square birds," and the third generation of birds from 1961 to 1963. The 1955–1957 Chevys, the tail-finned Caddys climaxing in the 1959–1960 Cadillac (batmobiles!). How many people out there secretly fondle a 1959 Cadillac convertible in their dreams? Come on, be honest!

Almost any car from the "golden age" of 1955–1960 fits the dream machine, according to this book's definition. For here, a few models from the 1940s and the 1970s had to be included because they meant so much to the dream machine era. The bottom line is, if you love it, it is a "dream car." A dream machine makes one's heart beat a little faster, stirs the imagination, brings a silly grin to the face, and brings a slight sense of euphoria.

Detroit's dream machines were special or prototype cars that were made for their shows, for the motoramas, where they unveiled new car models. Usually when the new style changeover came, a manufacturer had one dream machine of some possible future car alongside the complete line of new models. They were also known as futurama cars. This book does not pertain to those cars!

Dream machines in this book are real cars. They are fun cars to drive and own. They are "a good feeling, I own it type of car and you don't but wish you did, doesn't it bring back memories, my father owned one, we got married in one, we broke down in Florida and made it back to New York with a bad generator, built like a tank type of car!"

The reasons that the people whose cars I photographed own them are as varied as the cars they own. The two basic reasons are: they like the way the car looks and/or the memories the car brings with it. Some of the people are too young to have any recollection of the car when it was new; they just like the way it looks.

The cars owned by Dan and Fred Kanter range from a 1951 Nash to a 1955 Packard Caribbean convertible to a 1963 Ghia. Dan and Fred like all old cars, but Packards are their favorites. They bought their first Packard in 1960—two years after Packard ceased to exist (really four years, since the 1957–1958 models were really a hybrid Studebaker called Packardbakers). Now how can they buy a Packard in 1960 and keep buying Packards (Dan drives a 1955 Clipper daily)? Since Packard was no

longer making parts, Dan and Fred started buying all the old parts they could, then they started making parts. Today they are the world's largest supplier of Packard parts. There is no reason why a 1949 Packard should not be around 100 years from now and not in a museum but on the road.

The Kanters not only supply Packard parts, they have parts for most other cars also. They are truly car nuts! The people who work for them are also car crazy. Mike Gadjek drives a 1941 Hudson, not occasionally but daily. When he feels like "stepping out a bit," he moves up to his 1960 Rambler, or 1950 Hudson.

There will be no judgments on the beauty or nonbeauty of the cars that follow. The people who own them love them, and I hope you do too. Many of these cars have memories stored inside them for their owners.

The cars were designed by people for people. They were expressions of individuality that their owners carry on today.

So enjoy, don't take it too seriously, and maybe you'll find your dream machine on the following pages.

The Dream Machines

Somewhere between 1948 and 1968 there did exist an American dream machine. It was the 1950 Mercury coupe—the James Dean car; the 1951 Ford; the 1955 Chevy; the 1954 Mercury Sun Valley; the 1955 Ford Crown Victoria; the original two-seat T-Bird and Corvette; the first Mustangs (1965–1966); the G.T.O.; and the Batmobile Cadillac!

Even the humble station wagons were there . . . the 1955–1957 Chevy Nomads and Pontiac Safaris, and the woodie wagons.

Why this time period? What is so special about this era, especially the period from 1955 to 1965? Part of the lure is nostalgia, remembering the good and forgetting the not so good. But for the most part, it is the people who admire and collect these cars. The words that pop up the most often in conversations among car nuts seem to be "interesting, personality, a fun kind of car, it's mine," and one phrase that stands out is: "it's me, that car is me!"

In essence, these cars have soul and spirit. They are personal because they were designed by people for people. Take a good look at the interior of the 1952 Packard. That is not ergonomics or computerese, that is an interior of a car designed by a person for a person! That 1954 Studebaker is human technology, not computer science!

Prior to World War II, cars were still one step beyond "every person's dreams." After the war, as the economy boomed, a Chevy convertible or Mercury coupe was not beyond one's imagination. A "rocket" Olds 88 was a reality.

Automobiles hit full stride in this period. There are people who will insist it was the period from the late 1920s until 1940, the so-called "classic period," that cars were at their best—this feeling is more nostalgia than truth. Many of those pre-war cars were cumbersome to drive: heavy steering, poor braking, windshield wipers that were inadequate (vacuum-powered), poor ventilation, poor heating.

The postwar cars were as simple to operate as their prewar cousins, but had more power and were more economical. The arrival of the V-8 (which Cadillac introduced in 1916); automatic transmission; air conditioning (first introduced by Packard in 1939); all these came into their own in the 50s. This period was marked by a variety of advances among automakers.

One of the most popular cars of the Golden Age is the 1955–1957 Chevy. It can hold six people and their luggage, cruise all day at 65 mph and deliver 20-25 mpg, depending on engine set-up. No plastic, all steel, no frills, and $2,100.

If you happen to be stopped at a gas station and the car next to you starts to make a "whistling" sound, chances are it is a 1949 Packard. When the gas tank starts to approach "full," a whistle would start to go off letting the attendant (or you) know to cut off the flow of gas, not only to prevent waste, but to stop the overflowing of gasoline onto the chrome or paint of the car.

The 1949 line-up of Chrysler Corporation cars had as an option ($1.00) a funny-looking object (nipple) at the rear of the passenger-side fender right next to the lid of the trunk. This little device enabled the owner to check the spare tire pressure without opening the trunk, or removing anything near the spare to do so.

The 1938 Oldsmobile convertible had a special vacuum-operated radio. As the car's speed increased, the volume of the radio got louder. As the car slowed down, the volume went down also. As the wind noise grew louder from the car going faster, the special vacuum radio compensated for this with a gadget that was hooked to the gas pedal, so as gas pressure was increased (more wind noise also), the volume grew louder.

By the mid 50s the U.S. auto industry was starting to get into full stride design-wise. The effects of the Korean war and World War II were behind.

To celebrate its fiftieth anniversary in 1953, GM brought out three limited-production luxury convertibles—the Buick Skylark, the Cadillac Eldorado, and the Oldsmobile Fiesta. These cars ranged in price from $5,000 for the Buick to $7,000 for the Eldorado. Among the Eldorado's features were a completely automatic top that disappeared under its own metal cover, and electric heaters in the front seat to keep you warm until the whole car warmed up.

Small conveniences like these were not new to Cadillac or other luxury cars of the period. Cadillac offered its customers power windows, power antenna, power seat, automatic transmission, a V-8 engine under the hood and a sunroof overhead in their 1941 Fleetwood long before most other carmakers.

In 1954 Chevrolet brought out their famous Corvette—the first and still only true American sports car. Knight Rider, move over—long before you were on a drawing board there was the TV series _Route 66_ with its two male stars cruising around in their 1957 red Corvette.

Not to be outclassed, T-Bird had as its star the 1957 model in 77 _Sunset Strip_. Twenty-five years later the popular series _Simon & Simon_ has its two male leads cruising around San Diego in a 1957 Chevy convertible. The cars of the 50s caused a commotion when they were new; they do the same when they are old.

In 1955, the country was finally recovering from World War II and the Korean

conflict. The United States and the world were at peace, the economy was healthy, and the U.S. auto industry had fresh styling and improved mechanics. The public responded by buying over 9,000,000 U.S.-made vehicles—something the public has not done since. There have been years when more cars were sold, but not U.S.-made cars.

So popular was 1955 and the five-year period following, that it is probably the most collectible period as far as old cars are concerned for today. It was a milestone in U.S. car history. Every make had a new face and mechanics to go along with the styling. The V-8 engine arrived along with automatic transmission, seat belts, and most power accessories that are available today. Almost all makes had the 12-volt electrical system. By 1957 all would change over to this voltage. From air conditioning to power steering to seat belts with shoulder harness, you could buy a Ford or a Caddy equipped with any or all power options.

The year 1955 also saw the birth of the 2-seat Thunderbird, a car that needs no explanation. It is as exciting to look at today as it was exciting in 1955. It was also the second year for the Corvette—a car which still holds true to its original idea and concept. In 1955, the Vette got a V-8, increasing its appeal.

Every year until 1960, cars grew a little chromier, with more power options. Fins grew finnier until they climaxed in 1959/1960 to the ultimate with Cadillacs who started the whole fin business in 1948.

As for power, the 1957 Corvette was able to go from 0 to 60 mph in 6.1 seconds with a top speed of 135 + . The 1959 Lincoln Continental, weighing 5,200 lbs, went from 0 to 60 in 9 seconds and was as comfortable as a living room club chair besides. The Cadillac was only one second slower.

In year 1958, foreign car sales totaled only 4 percent of all cars sold in the

United States. These were European cars, there were no Japanese cars . . . yet. There wasn't even sushi!

Jim Nance of Ford Motor Company, when asked about the foreign car and the small economy car in an interview in 1958, said, "If foreign car sales hit 5 percent, Ford may be interested in tooling up for a small economy car. But the American car buyer really wants his car big, so I cannot see that happening too soon." In 1959 foreign car sales shot up to 11 percent!

Until then, American manufacturers never had an interest (except for some mavericks such as Powell Crosley, Henry Kaiser, and American Motors headed by George Romney) in making a small economy car. The profits were greater in big luxury-type cars. But as their share of the total auto market kept dwindling, they finally changed over. Unfortunately for them that was twenty years after the fact.

When the smaller, more economical car (most luxury cars were economical too; it is a misconception about their gas-guzzling ways) grew larger that is when trouble started on the American auto front. Except for Rambler (American Motors) and Studebaker, no U.S. auto company was paying any attention to this market in the 1950s—not among the big three anyway. There were small independents, but they lacked the dealerships the big three had. One foreign maker, however, did pay attention . . . the name, Volkswagen; the car, the Beetle.

There were many people who wanted a basically cheap (as in not much money) car. There were some available through the mid-50s in the form of the 150 Chevy and Ford Mainline series. But they grew fancier and more expensive as the decade grew to a close. The people who wanted a basic transportation car were not necessarily poor. They just wanted a car to get them around. It was not offered domestically so they turned to European makers. Domestic car makers were trying to ignore these small cars and convince buyers through advertising to think big.

For highway driving and long trips it was hard to beat an American "Yank Tank." But obviously there were people who did not need or want this type of car. By 1960, panic struck the automakers and the Corvair, Falcon, and Valiant appeared (GM, Ford, Chrysler). Within a few years they were bulked up until they were more of an intermediate car than a compact. This is a contradiction but it was not all the fault of the auto industry. Given the choice in these days the American driver would rather have a bigger car than a smaller one, if he could afford it. The "performance" that the European cars promised usually meant gas economy coupled with "feeling the road," a euphemism used for feeling every rut and pothole, being jostled through turns, feeling the wind rock the car, and hearing the wind rather than the radio.

Ever notice how people with small cars think 60 miles is a trip? How they seem to complain about back trouble? How people with "big" cars think nothing of going away for a few days, even when it means sitting in the car for three hours or more? Such was the appeal then of American cars versus European, and the quandary that the auto industry could not figure out.

The early 60s saw a "cleaning up" of American cars. Fins disappeared and the compact car appeared en masse. The Pontiac Tempest of 1961–1963 was one of these compacts. It was a 4-cylinder engine with independent suspension on all four wheels and the transmission mounted in the rear. It had 50/50 weight distribution . . . 50 percent over the front wheels, 50 percent over the rear wheels. It could get 20-25 mpg and had a 20-gallon fuel tank. The radiator could come out in ten minutes, the water pump fifteen minutes. The car was too simple to be true. The 1964 Tempest went back to conventional suspension and the transmission was once again placed in the front with the drive shaft connected to the rear wheels.

The only other car to have such a set-up as the 1961–1963 Tempests is the Porsche 928 which cost over $40,000! in 1977! The Tempest was $2,600 in 1963. (In 1963 a rear-engined Porsche cost $3,000.)

The year 1964 saw the ushering in of the muscle car and the famous pony cars. Pontiac took their Tempest body, put a 389 V-8 in it, gave it a firmer suspension and the G.T.O. was born. In late 1964, Ford brought out their classic Mustang, the first "pony car." Some people swear these Mustangs are living beings and that they breed, because there seems to be more on the road today than in 1965!

But 1964 also brought the last of tail fins. Appropriately, Cadillac laid the fin to rest. It was the first car sporting fins and the last one. It was the first year of the new Cadillac engine, the 429 cid V-8, going from 0 to 60 mph in 8 seconds, 0 to 100 in 22 seconds and topped out at 118 mph. With the air conditioning on, the car was clocked at 100 mph for 75 miles straight at Daytona without the slightest vibration or mechanical failure. As for gas mileage it got 12-17 mpg depending upon road conditions.

All Cadillac windows were power-operated (including the vent windows) and they all recessed completely, front and back. In emissions test in New York, a

1964 Cadillac, without any so-called pollution controls, exceeded the 1985 limits set by the state.

In 1961 Lincoln brought out their famous suicide or center-opening-door Continental. This car was (and still is) a refreshing change from the previous bulky Lincolns. It set a styling trend for luxury cars. The car was over a foot and a half shorter than the 1960 Continental.

The 60s saw the popularity of the "pony cars," the Mustang, Camaro, Firebird, Barracuda, and AMX, and their cousin the muscle car. The tail end of the 60s, on the other hand, saw the rise in popularity of the smaller, cheaper foreign car. Cars were changing, getting a little less exciting.

A friend sums it up best in his view, "When rear windows ceased to go down, station wagons had liftgates instead of tailgates, rear view mirrors were glued to the windshield instead of screwed into the roof and curved glass became the vogue, I lost interest." Ever hit your head on the curved glass on a door, or have your rear view mirror fall off as you adjusted it?

As another friend who owns a 1959 Buick convertible said, "There is absolutely no redeeming social value in this car and it will not help cure the common cold. But in the summer the kids (who are grown) ask to go for a ride and my wife said if I ever get rid of the car I should get my toothbrush and never come back. When we pull up to Hershey in the fall and see all that old tin on the horizon and over 200,000 crazies [at the Hershey auto show] like us, I know I got motor oil in my veins instead of blood!"

"They don't make them like they used to." We hear that expression a lot. On page 16 is a breakdown of the model year 1953 and what went into cars then. I tried to get a breakdown on cars from the 80s, but the manufacturers no longer keep records of this sort (at least so they say). Ford and Chrysler did not respond when asked about this; GM did more than respond; they sent more information than I bargained for. It is highly technical and I would need a few engineering people to help me break down all the different terms and code names. But taking into consideration many new cars do not have chrome bumpers, and do have plastic liners under the fenders, etc., the information that follows is interesting.

Taking an average weight of 3,800 lbs. (for 1953 cars) you can see exactly what went into a car. Numbers will represent pounds. The group miscellaneous includes antimony, molybdenum, nickel, tin, cork, tungsten, asbestos, mica, vanadium, and PLASTICS . . .

STEEL	2,556
GRAY IRON	521
MALLEABLE IRON	100
ALUMINUM AND ALLOYS	11
COPPER	26
COPPER ALLOYS	16
LEAD AND ALLOYS	30
ZINC AND ALLOYS	66
CHROMIUM	6
MANGANESE	19
SILICON	17
FABRIC	92
GLASS	76
LUBRICANTS	15
PAPER	55
RUBBER COMPOUND	206
SOUND DEADENER	11
MISCELLANEOUS	12 (this includes plastics!)
TOTAL	3,835

This is not to say that all 1953 cars weighed 3,835 lbs, this is just an average of all cars sold that year. A Plymouth weighed 3,007 lbs while a Packard weighed 4,190 lbs. A Chevrolet weighed 3,215 lbs and a Chrysler Crown weighed 4,425 lbs.

So the average car in 1953 had over 3,200 lbs of steel and iron in its makeup. That is more than many cars will weigh in 1985. Over 85 percent of the 1953 car was comprised of steel and iron.

One more thing . . . when speaking with people from the big three, only at GM did the person on the other end of the phone have a sense of humor and say, "we don't make them like that anymore, it is a changing world."

1941 *Hudson*

"Last Hudson and Built to Last!" So read a sign held by Hudson automobile workers above a 1941 Hudson to proclaim the start of wartime production and an end to civilian car-making for the time being.

Specifications

Factory Price	$1,500	
Overall Length	207"	
Height	64.5"	
Width	77"	
Weight	3,235 lbs.	
Engine	L-head 8 cyl	L-head 6 cyl
	254 cid	212 cid
Bore & Stroke	3 × 4	3 × 5
Compression	5.6:1	6.5:1
Horsepower	128 @ 4,200 rpm	103 @
Wheelbase	121"	4,000 rpm
Fuel Tank	20 gallons	
Cooling System	18½ qts	
Tires	6.50 × 15 (6.00 × 16)	
Electrical	6 volts	
Carburetor	2 bbls	
Axle Ratio	4⅑:1 *or* 4⅚:1	
Transmission	3-speed manual	

Accessories*

Radio
Heater/Defroster
Electric Clock
Sliding Front Seat
Directional Signals

*Except for some luxury cars, many items we take for granted now were options. Not until the mid-50s did such items as heaters, defrosters, turn signals, etc., become "standard" items.

The sign was right. This 1941 Hudson is still going strong today. It's a total original, and driven every day.

One of the 1941 Hudson's unique features was the glide-away front seat. In two-door models the front seat would glide forward about six inches to facilitate entry to the rear. This in a car 5½ feet tall!

The 1941 Hudson marked the end of another era. Running boards were eliminated after the war. One of their deepest mourners was Hollywood. Bank robbers always spring onto the running board of the getaway car as it sped off. Postwar cars started to get lower. Instead of stepping straight in, you stepped down. Hudson started the step-down look in 1948.

But the car's dramatic career was far from over. From 1952 to 1954, the Hudson was king of stock-car racing. The engine was a straight six-cylinder with Twin H, dual carburetors.

1948 *Oldsmobile Sedanette*

In 1948 the sedanette, or fastback, was a style on the way out. The pillarless, hardtop convertible introduced the next year by Olds, Buick and Cadillac stayed in style until about the mid-1970s. And, of course, it's back in vogue today.

The older version of the pillared fastback had a trunk, unlike today's model. Its graceful tapered style made the sedan seem to glide through the air or over the road, combining easy elegance with roomy comfort.

Specifications

Factory Price	$2,600
Overall Length	213"
Height	64"
Width	77"
Weight	3,460
Engine	L-head straight 8 cyl 257 cid
Bore & Stroke	3.25 × 3.87
Compression	6.5:1
Horsepower	110 @ 4,600 rpm
Wheelbase	125"
Suspension	independent front, solid rear axle (coil front, leaf rear)
Fuel Tank	18 gals
Cooling System	12 qts
Tires	7.60 × 15
Electrical	6 volts
Carburetor	2 bbls
Transmission	3-speed manual hydramatic/optional

Accessories

Power Windows
Hydramatic (automatic transmission)
Heater/Defroster
Radio
Chrome Wheel Rings (beauty rings)
Rear Window Wiper
Fog Lamps
Spot Light
E-Z-Eye Glass
Windshield Washer
Back-Up Lights
Sunvisor

The popular Mustang of 1965–1966 had a fastback as one of their models. It seems almost every small car made from the late 1970s on has a fastback in its line-up. Do they really look better than the Olds Sedanette?

Cadillac and Buick stopped production on their sedanettes in 1950; Pontiac, Chevy and Oldsmobile in 1951.

1948 *Tucker*

T he Tucker Torpedo, the car with the center head-light that turned with the wheels, had a history as dramatic as its futuristic look. The car had a rear engine, four-wheel independent suspension, a permitter frame with a step-down floor and no drive-shaft tunnel, a foam-padded dash, a pop-out windshield, and the least drag of any car ever produced. The year? 1948!

Preston Tucker was an aggressive, visionary entrepreneur who dreamed of building the most advanced

22

Specifications

Factory Price	$2,500
Overall Length	219"
Height	60"
Width	77"
Weight	4,235
Engine	flat opposed 6 cyl/ohv (mounted in rear) 334.1" (L-head aluminum block)
Bore & Stroke	4.5 × 3.5
Compression	7.01:1
Horsepower	166 @ 3,000 rpm
Wheelbase	130"
Suspension	4-wheel independent front, equal A arms/rear, torsion unit
Fuel Tank	20 gal
Tires	7.00 × 15
Electrical	6 volts
Carburetor	2 bbls
Axle Ratio	3.3:1
Transmission	4-speed synchromesh/transaxle

car of its time. He did just that—only to be the victim of an unprecedented hatchet campaign that killed his car, his company, and ultimately, Tucker himself.

The story began at the end of World War II, when the postwar market for new cars was about to boom. If ever there was a time to introduce a new car to bring in a new era, it was then. Except for Studebaker, all the car manufacturers were planning to market warmed-up 1942 models.

In 1946 Tucker gathered together a group of like-minded Detroit automobile people and formed the Tucker Corporation. Their car was going to be fast, safe, long-lived and reliable. The Torpedo was all of those. It could hit 60 mph in ten seconds, and 100 mph in thirty-three seconds. Its top speed was 120 mph, although it was once clocked at 131. And with all that, its safety record exceeded any of today's.

The first Torpedo was to have a huge 589 cid flat-six liquid-cooled engine mounted crosswise in the rear. That engine would drive the Tucker at highway speeds while ticking over at a lazy 600 rpm. Because of the low rpm it was described as a lifetime engine and averaged 20 miles to the gallon.

Not surpisingly, the response to the car was overwhelming. The only problem seemed to be how to build enough of them to meet the demand. But success of this magnitude caused more than a little concern with the Detroit establishment.

What Tucker was subjected to would have broken a lesser person early on. To make a long story short, they placed every possible obstacle in his path when he attempted to buy steel, machine tools, and all the ancillary materials necessary to manufacture automobiles on a large scale. When he finally succeeded in overcoming these obstacles he was attacked in the courts through an

Accessories
Radio
Heater/Defroster
Whitewall Tires
Pop-Out Front Windshield

SEC investigation instigated by Senator Homer Ferguson of Michigan.

Tucker was eventually cleared of all charges, but the continual harrassment finally took its toll. During the time he was defending himself his company's expenses rolled on. Eroding capital put an end to the corporation. The Establishment finally won, and Tucker died shortly after, in 1955.

Forty-nine Tuckers were built before production was stopped and these are all registered today by their cultist owners. One man in Pennsylvania owns three!

1949 *Kaiser Virginian*

H enry J. Kaiser, started out as a shipbuilder (Kaiser Industries). After the war he decided to get into the automobile business along with Joe Frazier (formerly with Graham Paige, a defunct auto maker of the prewar period).

The 1949 Kaiser Virginian displayed the Kaiser genius. With this car he introduced ''hardtop'' styling to four-door models years before the big three car makers would. When the windows were rolled down in the Virginian, the

26

Specifications

Factory Price	$3,000
Overall Length	206.5″
Height	62″
Width	74″
Weight	3,541
Engine	in line L-head six 226.2 cid
Bore & Stroke	$3^{15}/_{15} \times 4^{3}/_{8}$
Compression	7.3:1
Horsepower	100 @ 3,600 rpm
Wheelbase	123½″
Suspension	independent front/solid rear axle
Fuel Tank	17 gals
Cooling System	14 qts
Tires	7.10 × 15
Electrical	6 volts
Carburetor	1 bbl

Accessories

Heater/Defroster
Electric Clock
Outside Mirror Driver's Side
Radio
Spare Tire
Trip Odometer
Fuel and Temperature Gauges
Leather Interior
Nylon Roof either black or tan
Fender Skirts standard option, unless asked to delete

glass pillar between the front and rear doors could be slipped out to create the hardtop open-air feeling attained in the prewar period with the 4-door convertible.

In mid-1949 and 1950 the handsome, sporty Virginian style was also offered in a true four-door convertible.

Kaiser also introduced the forerunner of today's hatchback—the Traveler or utility wagon. The Traveler's trunk (similar to the Desoto model) was hinged in the middle, so that the bottom half folded downward and the top lifted up. The rear seat could then fold down to create a flat cargo area that extended from the back of the front seat to the end of the car. From a six-passenger vehicle with a closed trunk the Traveler ingeniously turned into a utility wagon with a cargo area more than six feet long.

Kaiser's Henry J was marketed soon after (1952–1954) and was sold through the Sears chain as the Allstate. At 182″ long with a 4- or 6-cyl engine (134 or 161 cid), it was too small and economical for that (expansive) time period.

Model year 1955 would see the end of the Kaiser, in the U.S. anyway; the cars were produced in Argentina until 1962. Among the "small" safety items Kaiser introduced were the wrap around taillight which served both as a stoplight and side safety marker. The 1952–1955 models sported this light. The cars also offered a full instrument panel crash pad years before they became mandated by the government.

1949 *Buick Roadmaster*

Portholes! Those four holes on the fender would become a Buick trademark (later to shift from fender to hood and back). Along with the gunsight hood ornament introduced in 1947, the distinctive portholes (four on the Roadmaster, three on the lesser Buick models) still stand for the Buick image today.

The taillights that shine from the rear fenders were another unique feature of the 1949 Buick. The same year saw Dynaflow, the famed Buick automatic transmission, gain in popularity as the smoothest and possibly the slowest automatic ever made.

The Roadmaster was a car with a distinctive personality. It could be recognized coming or going—its rear by those unique taillights that were set into the rear fender, (and in model year 1949 only!) the snappy side portholes or the famous front grille), that open toothy look made the car seem always ready for a new adventure on

Specifications

Factory Price	$3,200
Overall Length	214" (Super and Special 209½")
Height	64"
Width	80" (Super and Special 77")
Weight	4,370 (Special sedan to Estate Wagon 4,115 to 4,500)
Engine	Roadmaster ohv/8 cyl 320.2 cid
Compression	6.9:1
Horsepower	150 @ 3,600 rpm
Wheelbase	126" (121" for Super and Special)
Suspension	all/independent front, solid rear axle
Bore & Stroke	3⁷/₁₆ × 4⁵/₁₆
Fuel Tank	19 gals/all
Cooling System	19 qts
Tires	8.20 × 15
Electrical	6 volts/all
Carburetor	2 bbls/all
Transmission	Dynaflow

Accessories

Automatic Transmission Dynaflow
Heater Defroster
Electric Clock
Power Seat 4 way
Outside Mirror with spotlight
Radio
Power Antenna/manual in center of windshield/ cranks down from inside
Rear-Window Defogger blower available on hardtop cars
Spare Tire
Trip Odometer
Fuel and Temperature Gauges
Power Windows
Leather Interior

the highways. Take a good look at that grille! This car is actually smiling at you. Next time you see one of these cars on the road, take a good look at the person behind the wheel. He's smiling too!

The Roadmaster was the top of the line for Buick in 1949. The lesser models were the Special and Super. The Estate Wagon or Woodie was higher priced than the Roadmaster Convertible and is worth just slightly less today.

The Special and Super line shared the same engine, a ohv/8 cyl (248 cid). In the Special, it put out 110 hp @ 3,600 rpm and in the Super 115 hp @ 3,600 rpm. Compression in the Special was 6.3:1 and in the Super 6.6:1. They both rode on a 121" wheelbase.

The Dynaflow was available only on the Roadmaster and Super.

1949 *Packard*

"Ask the man who owns one." It may sound chauvinistic but that was the Packard slogan from about 1905 until their demise in 1956. Supposedly one day someone had the audacity to ask Henry Joy (Joy bought Packard Motor from James Packard in 1901) how his cars were. Joy's reaction, "Ask the man who owns one!"

Among the Packard's unique features were the whistling gas tank. When the tank approached full, it would start to whistle. This would let the person know to

Specifications

Factory Price	$3,000
Overall Length	211¹¹⁄₁₆″
Height	64″
Width	77″
Weight	4,300
Engine	L-head in line, 8 cyl 327 cid
Bore & Stroke	3½ × 4¼
Compression	7:1
Horsepower	150 @ 3,600 rpm
Wheelbase	127″
Suspension	independent front (double-acting shock absorbers) rear/solid axle, semi-elliptic springs 54⅜″ long
Fuel Tank	20 gals (whistle warning when nearing full)
Cooling System	19 qts
Tires	8.20 × 15
Electrical	6 volts (some had optional 8 volts), 40 amp generator
Frame	X-member type, box section side rails
Carburetor	2 bbls
Axle Ratio	3.9:1
Transmission	standard/synchronized with overdrive optional

Accessories

Automatic Transmission Ultramatic, clutchless type of shift
Heater & Defroster
Electric Clock
Power Seat
Air Conditioning called all-season ventilation
Radio
Power Antenna
Rear Window Defogger
Spare Tire standard with optional check on exterior of car for tire pressure
Trip Odometer
Fuel & Temperature Gauges
Power Windows
Fuel Tank Whistle

turn off the flow of gas so as not to waste any and also to prevent any spillage onto the handrubbed paint or shiny chrome.

Another feature was the manual transmission, actually a semi-automatic. This was when the only cars with automatic were Buick, Cadillac and Oldsmobile. By pushing a button on the dashboard the process of depressing the clutch to shift was eliminated. No longer would fancy footwork be needed when going uphill and faced with a red light at the top of the hill. All one had to do was shift but without the clutch. The car was slightly less responsive but if the driver wanted quicker response all one had to do was pull out the button and, shifting through the gears, the clutch was activated.

Packard was always a quality car and a luxury car. Why its fall from glory? A man whose business is taxi meters offers this reasoning: after the war cars were in short supply (W.W. II) and great demand. Packard marketed their 7 passenger (with sunroof in the rear) for taxi service. When the well-to-do saw the Packard sporting a taxi light and yellow coat of paint they rushed to Cadillac.

The 1949 also had what some people refer to as the "bathtub" look (also used by Nash). You decide.

The optional hood ornament is a Cormorant. These are seabirds that are quite adept at catching fish.

1950 *Mercury Coupe*

James Dean did not pesonally own or drive this particular Mercury, but he did drive one in *Rebel Without a Cause*. This movie cemented the 1950 Merc into legend status overnight, and classic status forever!

The car (especially in black) seems to say to parents, and fathers in particular, "my daughter is not going out with the guy who drives this car." The 1950 Merc is a macho car. It is also a cleanly designed car which was ideal

Specifications

Factory Price	$2,000
Overall Length	206.8"
Height	63"
Width	73"
Weight	3,500
Engine	V-8 L-head
	255.4 cid
Bore & Stroke	3.19 × 4
Compression	6.80:1
Horsepower	110 @ 3,600 rpm
Wheelbase	118"
Suspension	independent front/rear leaf springs, solid axle
Fuel Tank	19 gals
Cooling System	22 qts
Tires	7.10 × 15
Electrical	6 volts
Carburetor	2 bbls
Axle Ratio	n/a
Transmission	3-speed manual/overdrive optional

Accessories

Radio
Heater/Defroster
Power Windows
Power Seat
Leather Interior
Padded Canvas or Vinyl Roof (Monterey Coupe)
Spare Tire

for customizing (as can be seen in the 1950 Mercury LEAD-SLED).

The 1949–1951 Mercury was basically the same body style. Whether it is through cars, clothes, or designers people try to achieve a "look." The 1949–1951 Mercury did just that. They had a look. Put that together with a jet black finish, a young, good looking, macho type guy, but with a touch of tenderness (the new man?), and a certain intangible, and you have the 1950 Mercury Coupe pictured here. Or the "James Dean Car!"

In 1955, James Dean died in a car crash. He was driving a 1955 Porsche Speedster.

1950 *Pontiac Sedan*

T he Indian chief Pontiac, whose head graced this car's hood, lights up when the car's exterior lights are on. This is not a customizer's trick, but a factory option!

If you could not afford that big, shiny black Buick, a

36

Specifications

Factory Price	$2,100	
Overall Length	202½"	
Height	63"	
Width	75¾"	
Weight	3,385/3,415 (6 cyl)	3,475/3,480 (8 cyl)
Engine	L-head 6 cyl 239.2 cid	L-head 8 cyl 248.9 cid
Bore & Stroke	3⁹⁄₁₆ × 4	4¼ × 4¾
Compression	6.5:1	715:1
Horsepower	90 @ 3,400 rpm	103 @ 3,800 rpm
Wheelbase	120"	
Suspension	independent front/solid rear axle	
Fuel Tank	17½ gals	19¾ qts
Cooling System	18 qts	
Tires	7.60 × 15	
Electrical	6 volts	
Frame	n/a	
Carburetor	1 bbl	
Axle Ratio	4.1:1/3.9:1/4.3:1/hydramatic 3.63:1	
Transmission	3-speed synchromesh (manual) hydramatic optional (4-speed automatic)	

Accessories

Radio
Heater/Defroster
Windshield Sun Visor
Rear Fender Skirts
Remington Auto Home Shaver
Rear Window Wiper
Glove Compartment Light
Luggage Compartment Light
Safety Spotlight
Fog Lights
Venetian Blinds for rear window
Hood Trouble Light
Power Windows
Hydramatic automatic transmission
Windshield Washer

Pontiac was a nice consolation. The car was basically the same as the 1949 which was the first new design look for Pontiac since the close of World War II. This look would be carried over to 1951. In 1952 a more boxy look appeared. It would not be until 1955 that Pontiac would get a V-8. Whether it was the new V-8, the economy, or a new style change, the 1955 Pontiac sold 554,000 compared to 287,000 in 1954.

1951 *Nash Rambler Country Club*

The 1951 Country Club Coupe was the first successful compact introduced to the American buyer. It had style—it was a hardtop or pillarless car which only the top of the line cars had then—and it was roomy and economical. The car could deliver an honest 20-25 mpg.

The 1951 Country Club had front seats that could recline into a bed. What set the Rambler apart from other small cars at the time and contributed to its success was the fact it was really a small luxury car. There was nothing

38

Specifications

Factory Price	$2,000
Overall Length	176"
Height	59"
Width	73"
Weight	2,400
Engine	L-head in line 6 cyl 172.6 cid
Bore & Stroke	3⅛ × 3¾
Compression	7.25:1
Horsepower	82 @ 3,800 rpm
Wheelbase	100"
Suspension	independent front/leaf spring rear
Fuel Tank	20 gals
Cooling System	15 qts
Tires	5.90 × 15
Electrical	6 volts
Frame	unitbody construction
Carburetor	1 bbl
Transmission	manual/3-speed

Accessories

Radio
Electric Clock
Courtesy Lights
Power Antenna
Rear Window Wiper
Windshield Washer
Split Reclining Front Seat converts to bed
Fog Lights
Windshield Visor
Plastic Screens to put on windows to keep bugs
    out, if car was to be slept in overnight
Spotlight with Mirror
Heater/Defroster

cheap about its look or its interior. The Country Club was simply smaller and more compact than most of the other cars from the big three. It was fun to drive and economical besides. It seems like the Country Club was built more for the 80s than the early 50s.

In 1954 Nash introduced air conditioning that was practical and which helped revolutionize the air conditioning option. Nash was part of Kelvinator and put that knowledge in refrigeration to use for car air conditioning. The unit was able to fit under the hood rather than in the trunk. This small feat helped to bring air conditioning to the low-priced field and is the basis for all modern-day air conditioning units.

Nash was also the first to introduce fresh-air heating in 1937. Until then heaters just circulated the same stale air. The Nash heater brought fresh air in every minute to be warmed up and circulated.

In the 1958 NASCAR coast-to-coast economy run a Rambler with basically the same engine as that available in 1951 averaged 35.4 mpg from Los Angeles to Miami.

1952 *Packard Patrician 400*

P ackard advertised the 400 as "The Most Luxurious Motor Car in the World." Everything in the car pictured here is original, including the color combination.

The car promised comfort and luxury, from its club chair high seats to its spacious height of 63". One could enter the car with grace or a ten gallon hat. The passengers in the rear were treated to footrests which were a standard item.

Specifications

		200 series
Factory Price	$3,800	
Overall Length	218″	
Height	63″	
Width	78″	
Weight	4,100	
Engine	L-head in line 8 cyl.	L-head in line 8 cyl
	327 cid	288 cid
Bore & Stroke	3½ × 4¼	3½ × 4¼
Compression	7.3:1	7:1
Horsepower	150 @ 3,600 rpm	135 @ 3,600 rpm
Wheelbase	127″	
Suspension	independent front/rear leaf springs, solid axle	
Fuel Tank	20 gals	
Cooling System	19.9 qts	
Tires	8.00 × 15	
Electrical	6 volt	
Carburetor	2 bbls	
Transmission	Ultramatic (automatic) standard on Patrician manual with overdrive optional on 200 and 300 series	

Accessories

Power Steering
Power Brakes (Easamatic)
Automatic Transmission
Heater/Defroster
Electric Clock
Four-Way Power Seat
Outside Mirror Driver's Side (with spotlight)
Air Conditioning
Radio (signal seeking) with rear speaker
Rear Window Defogger (blower type)
Rear Window Wiper
Spare Tire
Trip Odometer
Full Instrumentation
Leather Upholstery
Curb Feelers
Underhood Lamp
Power Windows

The Patrician 400 is a one model line and the number refers to the so-called mythical 400 of society. It would be like saying rich and super rich, just an extra emphasis on the luxury of the car.

1953 *Buick Skylark*

To celebrate its 50th anniversary in 1953 Buick introduced its limited production Skylark. It was built on the Roadmaster chassis, but actually fit into the category of a custom car. Its windshield and upper torso were chopped and lowered as customizers would do to their own cars. Its beltline and overall height were "low"

45

Specifications

Factory Price	$5,000
Overall Length	208″
Height	60″
Width	79.9″
Weight	4,500
Engine	OHV V-8 322 cid
Bore & Stroke	4 × 3.2
Compression	8.5:1
Horsepower	188 @ 400 rpm
Wheelbase	125.5″
Suspension	independent front/solid rear axle
Fuel Tank	19 gals
Cooling System	18 qts
Tires	8.00 × 15
Electrical	12 volt
Frame	X frame
Carburetor	4 bbls
Transmission	Dynaflow (automatic)

Accessories

Power Steering
Power Brakes
Automatic Transmission
Heater/Defroster
Electric Clock
Six-Way Power Seat
Air Conditioning/not available on convertible
Automatic Headlight Dimmer
Radio
Power Antenna
Rear Window Defogger/not available on convertible
Spare Tire
Trip Odometer
Fuel and Temperature Gauges
Power Windows
Front Seat slides forward about five inches to facilitate ease of entry and exit for rear-seat passengers (2-door models)

for that time period. The car had a racy look with a European flair.

This was the first year Buick had the V-8 engine and the 322 cid V-8 was standard on the Skylark. It was a fully equipped car and its price of $5,000 reflected this. Among its features was the glide-away front seat. The front seat slid forward on a track when someone wished to enter the rear. The wheel wells were usually painted either red, white or black at the factory. Only 1,690 cars were made and they are prized collector cars today.

1953 *Kaiser Manhattan*

With a pop-out windshield and padded dash, the 1953 Kaiser was ahead of its time. It had safety features which were mandated by the government over a decade later. All the instrument controls were recessed below the crash pad area of the dash.

By 1953 the big three auto makers were finally getting into high gear in postwar production and design. Kaiser was still an unknown, in the car world. Add to that what some considered "radical" design and many car buyers

48

Specifications

Factory Price	$2,700
Overall Length	211"
Height	60.25"
Width	74.9"
Weight	3,210
Engine	L-head in line 6 cyl 226.2 cid
Bore & Stroke	$3\frac{5}{16} \times 4\frac{3}{8}$
Compression	7.3:1
Horsepower	118 @ 3,650 rpm
Wheelbase	118.5"
Suspension	independent front/solid rear axle, leaf springs
Fuel Tank	17 gals
Cooling System	12.5 qts
Tires	71.0 × 15
Electrical	6 volts
Frame	n/a
Carburetor	2 bbls
Transmission	manual standard overdrive/optional Hydramatic/optional

Accessories

Power Steering
Power Brakes
Automatic Transmission/Hydramatic
Heater & Defroster
Electric Clock
Outside Mirror Driver's Side
Air Conditioning
Radio with rear speaker
Power Antenna
Rear Window Defogger
Spare Tire
Trip Odometer
Fuel and Temperature Gauges
E-Z-Eye Tinted Glass

were not willing to be the "first" to own these well made and proportioned cars. Kaiser would only last two more years. But in their legacy would be the first "personal" luxury car in the form of the Kaiser Darrin introduced in 1954, and the Henry J, one of the first small economical cars. Henry Kaiser had vision but he was two decades too soon.

1953 *Oldsmobile 88*

For the first time ever Oldsmobiles came equipped with the new 12 volt electrical system. By 1955 all cars would be made this way.

During the model year Oldsmobile had a fire at its Hydramatic plant and Dynaflow transmissions were used in many Oldsmobiles in place of the Hydramatic. The Oldsmobile pictured here is an early production model and came equipped from the factory with the Hydramatic.

Oldsmobile introduced the automatic transmis-

Specifications

Factory Price	$2,600
Overall Length	204"
Height	63"
Width	77"
Weight	3,531
Engine	OHV V-8
	303.73 cid
Bore & Stroke	3¾ × 3⁷⁄₁₆
Compression	8.0:1
Horsepower	165 @ 3,600 rpm
Wheelbase	120"
Suspension	independent front/solid rear axle
Fuel Tank	18 gals
Cooling System	21.5 qts
Tires	7.60 × 15
Electrical	12 volts
Frame	X frame
Carburetor	4 bbls
Transmission	manual standard Hydramatic/optional

Accessories

Power Steering
Power Brakes
Automatic Transmission Hydramatic
Heater & Defroster
Electric Clock
Six-Way Power Seat
Outside Mirror Driver's Side
Air Conditioning sedans only not convertible
Automatic Headlight Dimmer
Radio
Power Antenna
Rear Window Defogger
Full-size spare
Trip Odometer
Fuel and Temperature Gauges
Power Windows
Fiesta Hubcaps
Leather Interior
Canvas Top

sion in the form of its Hydramatic in 1939 to the motor world. In the 30s Oldsmobile also offered a vacuum radio (on convertibles) that got louder as the car went faster and grew lower as the car slowed down.

Ransom Eli Olds started his company in 1897. He sold out in 1904 to partner Samuel Smith because of policy differences between the two men. Though Olds could not use his personal name in starting a new company (he sold the company name along with the company) he could use his initials. That is the basis for the REO (Ransom Eli Olds) motor car company. REO produced cars and trucks. REO became Diamond REO in the 30s.

In addition to the motor car companies there is also a song named after Olds, "Merry Oldsmobile." A popular rock group of the 70s and 80s took their name from another Olds vehicle . . . a truck that was called a "speedwagon." Reo Speedwagon is the group's name. REO or just plain Olds, the name keeps rolling on.

1954 *Kaiser Darrin*

S liding doors, fiberglass body, and a totally un-Detroit look. The 1954 Kaiser Darrin was devoid of chrome in the chrome age! It had the tiniest of grilles when huge chrome grilles were as integral part of a car as the engine was.

Howard "Dutch" Darrin was a designer whose work went back to the 30s. One of his more famous designs was the prewar classic 1942 Packard Darrin. Before the age of computers and "ergonomics," people designed cars for

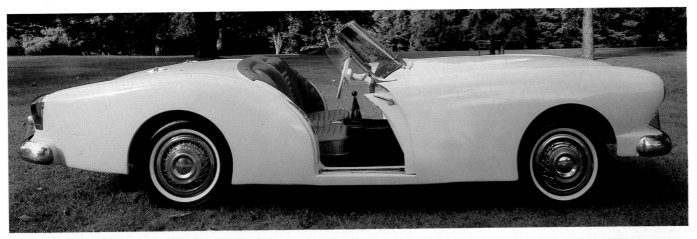

Specifications

Factory Price	$3,700
Overall Length	184"
Height	51" (with top up)
Width	67.56"
Weight	2,175
Engine	F-head in line 6 cyl (overhead inlet, side exhaust)
Bore & Stroke	3.12 × 3.50
Compression	7.6:1
Displacement	161 cu in
Horsepower	90 @ 4,200 rpm
Wheelbase	100"
Suspension	independent front/solid rear axle, leaf springs
Fuel Tank	13 gals (20 mpg)
Cooling System	12 qts
Tires	5.90 × 15
Electrical	6 volts
Carburetor	1 bbl
Axle Ratio	4.10:1
Transmission	manual with overdrive optional (Synchromesh) Hydramatic/optional
Body	fiberglass, metal frame
Sliding Doors/slide into front fenders	

people and Dutch Darrin was one of the best designers.

Unfortunately Kaiser was in financial trouble, the Darrin cost $3,700 and six months prior to its unveiling the Corvette was introduced at $3,500. Corvette sold 3,064; the Darrin 435. Production was halted.

Accessories

Radio
Heater/Defroster
Hydramatic Automatic Transmission
Leather Interior

The Darrin was a "personal luxury" car long before the phrase became a catchword. It was also a "pony car" at the same time. It was not a sports car. It was a sporty two-seat car that was simple to operate, service and maintain. The Darrin was everything but successful.

Today in the auto industry one of the "hot" vehicles is the utility van featuring its sliding side door. The Kaiser Darrin had two sliding doors in 1954.

1954 *Studebaker Starliner*

In 1953 Studebaker celebrated its centennial (they originally produced Conestoga wagons) and to celebrate Raymond Loewy designed the new line-up of Studebakers with "European Styling."

The 1954 line-up was identical to the 1953's. The name Starliner applied to the two-door hardtop. It was a revolutionary low car, being less than five feet high (56.25"); compared to other cars of this period this was LOW. The sleek, clean chrome-less styling has a timeless beauty that still holds up today.

Raymond Loewy was a design genius in the class of Dutch Darrin and Gordon Buehrig. Studebaker would give him two more projects to put his design genius into in the

Specifications

Factory Price	$2,300	
Overall Length	202″	
Height	56.25″	
Width	70.5″	
Weight	3,200	
Engine	OHV V-8	L-head 6 cyl
	232.6 cid	169.6″
Bore & Stroke	3⅜ × 3¼	3 × 4
Compression	7.5:1	7.5:1
Horsepower	120 @ 4,000 rpm	85 @ 4,000 rpm
Wheelbase	120″	
Fuel Tank	18 gals	
Cooling System	17¼ qts	10 qts
Tires	7.10 × 15	
Electrical	6 volts	
Carburetor	2 bbls	1 bbl
Transmission	3-speed manual overdrive/optional automatic/optional	

early 1960s. The cars would be the Gran Turismo Hawk by Studebaker and the Studebaker Avanti, which is still being made today as the Avanti II.

One of the features of the Studebaker was the Manual Transmission with Hill Holder. This was a device that enabled one to stop on a hill without keeping one foot on the clutch and the other on the brake and when the time came to shift into gear, you needed another foot for the gas pedal. The Hill Holder simply provided braking power on a hill so one could shift into gear safely without the worry of rolling backwards, downhill!

Another unique feature was the power antenna. It was manually controlled rather than motor power. By turning a knob you either raised or lowered the antenna. No worry of a motor ever burning out.

Accessories

Radio
Heater/Defroster
Automatic Transmission
Power Steering
Power Brakes
Spotlight
Power Antenna manually controlled. By turning a
    knob the antenna would retract. No worry
    about a motor burning out.
Kleenex Dispenser
Wire-Wheel
Clock
Underhood Light
Rear Window Defroster
Windshield Washer

1954 *Lincoln Capri*

I magine 98 mph for almost 2,000 miles! Jaguar, Mercedes, you say? No. The answer is the stock 1952–1954 Lincoln.

During the early 1950s there was a race called The Mexican Road Race also known as the Pan American Road Race. It stretched from Tuxtla, Mexico, near the Guatemale border to Juarez, across the Rio Grande from El Paso, Texas. The distance—1,933 miles, with altitudes from sea level to 10,380 above sea level. Lincoln won the event

Specifications

Factory Price	$3,900
Overall Length	214.8"
Height	62.7"
Width	77.4"
Weight	4,250
Engine	OHV V-8 cyl 317.5 cid
Bore & Stroke	3.8 × 3.5
Compression	8.0:1
Horsepower	205 @ 4,200 rpm
Wheelbase	123"
Suspension	front, ball joint, individual coil rear, solid axle, leaf springs
Fuel Tank	20 gals
Cooling System	22.5 qts
Tires	8.00 × 15 (convertible 8.20 × 15)
Electrical	12 volts
Carburetor	4 bbls
Transmission	Hydramatic (from GM, the next year Lincoln would produce their own)

Accessories

Power Steering
Power Brakes
Automatic Transmission/Hydramatic
Heater/Defroster
Electric Clock
Four-Way Power Seat
Outside Mirror Driver's Side
Radio with rear speaker
Power Antenna
Rear Window Defogger blower type
Spare Tire
Fuel and Temperature Gauges
Power Windows

three years straight, 1952–1954. In 1952 and 1953 Lincoln captured first, second, third and fourth place. In 1954 Lincoln took first and second. After 1954, the race was discontinued.

The course was over mostly rough terrain. To put it into modern day perspective: every city has its so-called "horror road." Not just a street but a major highway that destroys vehicles. There are usually abandoned cars strewn about such highways. In New York City it is called the FDR Drive. It circles Manhattan. The Mexican Road Race would be akin to staying on the drive (in whatever city) for 2,000 miles and averaging 98 mph. For the final stretch from Chihuahua to Juarez the lead Lincoln averaged 114 mph!

A safety note that can be applied today. The drivers were chosen by Lincoln because of their records as "smooth drivers." That is "instead of manhandling a car around a turn," these pilots put their cars into a curve as smoothly as possible. There's none of the swerving and jamming on of brakes that suggest a driver is over their head (or into peeling of rubber). Smooth driving saves rubber and brakes. It gets you through the turns faster and gives you a margin for emergency maneuvering.

1954 *Cadillac Fleetwood 60*

Those bumpers! The famous bulletlike projectiles were as much part of the 50s Caddy as the celebrities who were always photographed getting in or out of them. After a while the bumpers were called "Dagmars," after the bosomy blond actress of 50s fame.

The air conditioner in the 1954 Caddy was located in the trunk and the vents were overhead inside the car. There were four outlets, one in the ceiling at each corner—almost an outlet per passenger. The entire car was evenly

61

Specifications

Factory Price	$5,600
Overall Length	227.4" (series 62 216)
Height	62.1"
Width	80"
Weight	4,600
Engine	OHV V-8
	331 cid
Bore & Stroke	$3^{13}/_{16} \times 3^{5}/_{8}$
Compression	8.25:1
Horsepower	230 @ 4,400 rpm
Wheelbase	133" (series 62 129)
Suspension	independent front/solid rear axle with leaf springs
Fuel Tank	20 gals
Cooling System	19.75 qts
Tires	8.20 × 15
Electrical	12 volts
Frame	X frame
Carburetor	4 bbls
Transmission	Hydramatic

Accessories

Power Steering
Power Brakes
Automatic Transmission
Heater/Defroster
Electric Clock
Four-Way Power Seat
Outside Mirror Driver's Side
Power Windows
Air Conditioning
Automatic Headlight Dimmer
Radio with rear speaker
Power Antenna
Rear Window Defogger blower type
Spare Tire
Trip Odometer
Fuel and Temperature Gauges
E-Z-Eye Safety Glass

cooled, and each passenger could regulate the nearest air jet for maximum comfort.

Cadillac also continued the tradition of "hiding" the gas cap. From 1947 until 1958 the gas cap was concealed under the rear light on the driver's side. That left an impressive clean sweep along the side to the tail fins.

1954 *Mercury Sun Valley*

The Plexiglas or bubble-top roof—Mercury and Ford had it as early as 1954–1956. But they didn't prove popular at that time and production was discontinued. Now, of course, the moonroof is part of auto vocabulary. The spacious and sporty Mercury Sun Valley was just the kind of vacation-ready car that lent itself to the sightseeing roof.

The Mercury was a middle-of-the-road car and the plexiglass roof was a way Ford thought it could distinguish

64

Specifications

Factory Price	$2,600
Overall Length	203.7"
Height	62.2"
Width	74.4"
Weight	3,535
Engine	OHV V-8
	256 cid
Bore & Stroke	3.62 × 3.10
Compression	7.50:1
Horsepower	162 @ 4,400 rpm
Wheelbase	118"
Suspension	independent front/solid rear axle
Fuel Tank	19 gals
Cooling System	20 qts
Tires	7.10 × 15
Electrical	6 volts
Carburetor	4 bbls
Transmission	3-speed manual overdrive optional Merc-O-Matic/optional (automatic)

Accessories

Power Steering
Power Brakes
Automatic Transmission
Heater/Defroster
Electric Clock
Four-Way Power Seat
Power Windows
Air Conditioning
Radio
Power Antenna
Rear Window Defogger
Spare Tire
Trip Odometer
Fuel and Temperature Gauges
Leather Interior

these cars. The Mercury was always a little brother to Lincoln or a big brother to Ford. One group that always appreciated the car though were customizers and hot rodders. The Mercury always lent itself to creative touches by individuals.

1955 *Chevy Bel Air*

I f ever there was a Year of the Car, it was 1955. All the car makers had new line-ups with not only new designs but also new mechanics and options. The modern auto age had begun.

More than nine million American-made vehicles were produced that year, a figure that hasn't been equaled since. It was the year of the two-seat T-Bird, the second year of the Corvette, and an unprecedented number of conveniences were available—air conditioning, power

67

Specifications

Factory Price	$2,100	
Overall Length	195.6"	
Height	62.1"	
Width	74"	
Weight	3,195	
Engine	OHV V-8	in line 6 cyl
	265 cid	235.5 cid
Bore & Stroke	3.75 × 3	3⁹/₁₆ × 3¹⁵/₁₆
Compression	8.0:1	7.5:1
Horsepower	162 @ 4,400 rpm	136 @ 4,200
Wheelbase	115"	
Suspension	independent front/solid rear axle leaf springs	
Fuel Tank	16 gals	
Cooling System	17 qts	
Tires	6.70 × 15	
Electrical	12 volts	
Carburetor	2 bbls	1 bbl
Axle Ratio	manual 3.7:1 (4.11:1/op) same automatic 3.55:1	
Transmission	manual/3-speed overdrive/optional automatic/optional	

steering, power brakes and windows, and so on, with V-8 power and smoothness. The 1955–1957 Chevys are among the most collectible cars of the postwar period. They are pleasing to the eye, easy to operate, and economical to drive. The popularity of the 1955–1957 era is such that on highways or car shows there are 45-year-old teenagers

Accessories

Power Steering
Power Brakes
Automatic Transmission
Heater/Defroster
Electric Clock
Four-Way Power Seat
Power Windows
Air Conditioning V-8 only
Radio with rear speaker
Power Antenna
Rear Window Defogger blower type
Spare Tire
Trip Odometer
Fuel and Temperature Gauges
Electric Shaver

with their Chevy or T-Bird alongside 19-year-olds with their nifty fifties dream machine.

In 1955, V-8 power was here in all makes. The Chevy Bel Air marked the first time Chevrolet had ever offered a V-8.

The engine on a 1985 Cadillac is 251 cid, the 1955 Chevy 265 cid. The cars are almost identical in both length and weight. What is that expression . . . the more things change, the more they stay the same?

The two-door hardtop was so popular that in mid-year Buick, Olds, and Cadillac introduced their own four-door hardtops. By 1956 all the auto manufacturers had one.

1955 *Ford Crown Victoria*

The Crown Victoria in all its elegance and splendor entered the scene in 1955. The distinctive stainless steel bar that wrapped around the roof and rear-deck styling gave the Vicky a look that stood alone even among Fords. An added option was the rare glass top on the front half of the roof, forward of the stainless bar. Add to that a two-tone paint, with the side molding dividing the lower half of the car from the color on top of it, and you have a truly nifty fifties Crown Victoria. The Crown Vic

70

always looked as if it was moving—even while standing still. Just a pair of dice over the rear view mirror and this car was ready to go.

Some Crown Victorias had the optional police engine, which was the 292 cid T-Bird engine that put out 198 hp.

Great American Dream Machines

Specifications

Factory Price	$2,400
Overall Length	198"
Height	61"
Width	76"
Weight	3,400
Engine**	272 cid OHV 6 cyl OHV V-8 223 cid
Bore & Stroke	3.62 × 3.30 3.62 × 3.60
Compression	7.6:1 (8.5:1 op) 7.2:1
Horsepower	162 @ 4,400 rpm 182 @ 4,400 rpm optional 115 @ 2,900 rpm
Wheelbase	115.5"
Suspension	independent front/solid rear axle
Fuel Tank	17 gals (station wagons 19 gals)
Cooling System	20 qts
Tires	6.70 × 15/7.10 × 15 wagons
Electrical	6 volts
Carburetor	V-8 single 2 bbls/4 bbls optional 6 cyl, 1 bbl
Axle Ratio	manual 3.78:1/overdrive 3.89:1/automatic 3.30:1 wagon 4.09:1 4.271:1 3.54:1
Transmission	manual 3-speed overdrive automatic
Exhaust System	with 4 bbls, dual exhaust
Independent Front Ball Joints	
Rear Solid Axle	

Accessories

Power Steering
Power Brakes
Automatic Transmission
Heater/Defroster
Electric Clock
Four-Way Power Seat
Outside Mirror Driver's Side
Power windows
Air Conditioning
Radio with rear speaker
Power Antenna
Rear Window Defogger blower type
Spare Tire
Fuel and Temperature Gauges
Two-tone Paint
Continental Tire
Skirts

1955 *Mercury Montclair*

T he mid-50s Mercury was a Macho car if ordered the proper way: the "Frenched" fenders extending over the headlights, the optional skirts, and to top off the low and long look, a Continental tire.

Unlike pervious Mercs, which were long on looks but not really performance cars, the 1955 could perform up to its snazzy image.

Add the wraparound windshield typical of the mid-50s and all the power conveniences you could want,

Specifications

Factory Price	$2,700
Overall Length	206.3" (station wagon, 202")
Height	58.6" (sedan 61.2", wagon 62.4", coupe 60.3")
Width	76.4"
Weight	3,500
Engine	292 V-8 292 cid
Bore & Stroke	3.75 × 3.30
Compression	7.6:1 optional 8.5:1
Horsepower	188 @ 4,400 rpm 198 @ 4,400 rpm
Wheelbase	119" (wagons 118")
Suspension	independent front, ball joint/ solid rear axle
Fuel Tank	18 gals
Cooling System	20 qts
Tires	7.60 × 15
Electrical	6 volts
Carburetor	4 bbls
Axle Ratio	manual 3.73:1 overdrive 4.09:1 automatic 3.15:1
Transmission	manual overdrive/optional automatic/optional

Accessories

Power Steering
Power Brakes
Automatic Transmission
Heater/Defroster
Electric Clock
Outside Mirror Driver's Side
Power Windows
Air Conditioning
Radio with rear speaker
Power Antenna
Rear Window Defogger blower type
Spare Tire
Power Windows
Fuel and Temperature Gauges
Fender Skirts
Two-tone Paint
Plexiglas Roof covered only the front passenger
    compartment.
Continental Tire

and here is one tough car! And, of course, two-tone paint just to make the car complete.

Mercury started doing to their 1955 models what individuals were doing for years, dressing up the basically well-proportioned car to give it some flash—a custom car prepared by the manufacturer. It must have proved popular because 326,000 Mercs were sold in 1955 as compared to 256,000 in 1954.

1955 *Packard Caribbean*

The tri-color coat of satin-sheen laquer accents the long-low look of this car that is an invitation to adventure. There is a 352 cid V-8 under the hood with two 4-barrel carburetors at your command.

In the truest sense of the word this car is indeed a "Land Yacht." If you seek more than mere motoring, the thrill of driving a thoroughbred—you belong in a Packard Caribbean.

Specifications

Factory Price	$6,000
Overall Length	218.5" (Clipper 214")
Height	61.7"
Width	78"
Weight	4,800
Engine	OHV V-8
	352 cid
Bore & Stoke	4 × 3.5
Compression	8.5:1
Horsepower	275 @ 4,800 rpm (260 @ 4,600 rpm in Patrician and 400)
Wheelbase	127" (Clipper 122")
Suspension	Torsion Bar all four wheels
Fuel Tank	20 gals
Cooling System	26 qts
Tires	8.00 × 15
Electrical	12 volts
Carburetor	2 × 4 bbls/Patrician and 400 single 4 bbls
Axle Ratio	3.23:1 (manual 3.9:1/overdrive 3.9:1)
Transmission	Twin Ultramatic (standard on Caribbean, Patrician, and 400)

Accessories

Power Steering
Power Brakes
Automatic Transmission
Heater/Defroster
Electric Clock
Power Seat four way
Outside Mirror Driver's Side
Power Windows
Air Conditioning
Radio with rear speaker
Power Antenna
Rear Window Defogger blower type
Spare Tire
Trip Odometer
Fuel and Temperature Gauges
Power Windows
Torsion Level Ride with Power-Actuated Leveling System keeps car on even keel no matter what the load (car has no springs)

The 1955–1956 Packards offered a V-8 for the first time in Packard's history. Packard offered V-12's in the 30s but never a V-8. The 1955–1956 models were exciting to look at and had many innovative features, among them the automatic load leveler that some luxury cars are now offering.

But this effort at a modern V-8 and styling was just a little too late. After 1956 there would be no more Packards. The name would continue for two more years but the car was really a Studebaker with a little different trim and the name Packard put on it or what some people refer to as a "Packardbaker."

1956 Packard 400

T alk about comfort. Sitting in a Packard of this era is like relaxing in a super-comfortable club chair. Your feet reach the floor at just the right angle. To see out the window you have only to move your eyes, not your entire head—the windshield has height, not slope. You sit upright, with just the right support for your back.

The instrument panel of the Packard has gauges to tell you when something is going wrong, not idiot lights to

Specifications

Factory Price	$5,200
Overall Length	218.5″
Height	62.3″ (Caribbean 61.7″)
Width	78″
Weight	4,200
Engine	OHV V-8
	374 cid
Bore & Stroke	$4\frac{1}{8} \times 3\frac{1}{2}$
Compression	10.00:1
Horsepower	290 with single 4 bbls
	310 with two 4 bbls set up
Wheelbase	127″
Suspension	Torsion bar full length of car
Fuel Tank	20 gals
Cooling System	26 qts
Tires	8.00 × 20
Electrical	12 volts
Carburetor	two 4 bbls on Caribbean (single 4 bbls on all others)
Axle Ratio	3.54:1
Transmission	Twin Ultramatic with electronic push-button standard on Caribbean (optional on Patrician and 400)
	Patrician and 400 column shift with Ultramatic

tell you that something is wrong, and that it's too late to do anything about it.

The 310 hp advanced Packard V-8 engine develops maximum torque of 405. This mighty driving force makes itself felt in the lightning takeoff and passing ability and its easy acceptance of sustained high-speed driving requirements.

Accessories

Power Steering
Power Brakes
Automatic Transmission
Heater/Defroster two outlets, one for front pass,
    one for rear pass
Electric Clock
Six-Way Power Seat
Power Windows
Air Conditioning only option not standard on
    Caribbean
Automatic Headlight Dimmer
Radio with rear speaker (signal seeking type)
Power Antenna dual on rear fenders
Rear Window Defogger blower type
Power Door Locks electrically operated
Spare Tire
Trip Odometer
Fuel and Temperature Gauges
Automatic Overdrive
Reversible Interior Seat Cushions reverse from
    leather to cloth
Seat Belts
Spotlights

To confuse people (there is no logical reason) Packard decided in 1955 to call their luxury edition 4-door the Patrician, as they always did, but took the 400 off the end and called their luxury edition 2-door hardtop the 400. In 1956 to confuse matters more there was a Caribbean hardtop as well as convertible. So you now had a luxury 2-door in the form of the 400 and a super luxury car in the form of the Caribbean hardtop. If ordered with the optional dual quad engine and leather interior the 400 and Caribbean were the same car except for the tri-color scheme of the Caribbean. Enough confusion for you?

Among some of the features of the Packard were electronic pushbutton ultramatic . . . there was no shift lever but push buttons located on the dash slightly to the right of the steering. Electric wires activated by the pushing of a button put the car into gear.

Besides the difference in engine size, the 1956 Packard differed from the 1955 in design slightly. The 1956's front fenders extended further out over the headlights and its hood and trunk were squarer whereas the 1955's hood and trunk were rounder. The stainless steel moulding on the 1956 400 is the full length of the car; on the 1955, only half.

1956 *Chevy Bel Air*

T here were some minor differences between the 1955 and 1956 Chevy Bel Air. The taillights were different, and the 1956 Chevy had the hidden gas cap—like the Cadillac, in the driver's-side taillight. The Chevy also had a V ornament on the hood and trunk.

Among the power options was the Power Pac, an optional 4-barrel carburetor with dual exhausts. In 1956 it was called the Monte Carlo, and it increased the hp to 205 @ 4,600 rpm, with compression of 9.25:1. Power Pac was a dealer-installed option. For safety, the 1956 Chevy not only offered seat belts but a shoulder harness as well. The trick was and still is to get people to use them!

At the time it was called the "Monte Carlo." But somehow the term "Power Pac," took over and that is what it is now called.

Specifications

Factory Price	$2,200	
Overall Length	197.5"	
Height	60.5"	
Width	73.4"	
Weight	3,293	
Engine	OHV V-8	in line 6 cyl
	265 cid	235.5 cid
Bore & Stroke	3.75 × 3	3⁹⁄₁₆ × 3¹⁵⁄₁₆
Compression	8.0:1	8.0:1
	162 @ 4,400 rpm/manual	140 @ 4,200 rpm
Horsepower	170 @ 4,400 rpm (Powerglide)	
Wheelbase	115	
Suspension	coil/front, semi-elliptic/rear	
Fuel Tank	16 gals	
Cooling System	17 qts	
Tires	6.70 × 15	
Electrical	12 volts	
Carburetor	2 bbls	one bbl
Axle Ratio	manual 3.7:1 (op 4.11:1)	
	automatic 3.55:1	
Transmission	manual	
	overdrive	
	automatic	

Accessories

Power Steering
Power Brakes
Automatic Transmission
Heater/Defroster
Electric Clock
Six-Way Power Seat
Outside Mirror Driver's Side
Power Windows
Air Conditioning V-8 only
Automatic Headlight Dimmer
Radio with rear speaker, signal seeking
Power Antenna
Rear Window Defogger blower type
Spare Tire
Trip Odometer
Fuel and Temperature Gauges
Locking Gas Cap
Wire Wheels
Spotlights
Electric Shaver
Skirts

1952 *Chrysler Imperial Parade Car*

I n 1952 Chrysler "lent" the City of New York their latest Chrysler Imperial. In 1955 Chrysler dropped the name "Chrysler" from Imperial in order to give the car a separate identity. The Imperial got a slightly different body style from the standard Chrysler in 1956 and, to celebrate this event, the Chrysler Corporation aked for the car back from the city to "rebody" it with a 1956 body. The car was then given back to the city as a gift.

Specifications

Factory Price	about $10,000
Overall Length	249"
Height	61.2" (with roof if there was a roof)
Width	78.8"
Weight	5,500 (approximate)
Engine	354 cid
	OHV V-8
Bore & Stroke	3.94 × 3.69
Compression	9.0:1
Horsepower	280 @ 4,600 rpm
Wheelbase	145.5" (the 1952 had 145", the 1956 149" (this is still a 1952 chassis)
Fuel Tank	21 gals
Cooling System	26 qts
Tires	8.90 × 15
Electrical	12 volts
Carburetor	4 bbls
Axle Ratio	3.54:1
Transmission	automatic

This car was stored in the Bronx and would have been forgotten but for Mayor Koch who rediscovered it and enlisted the Imperial as the official city parade car. The car is a basic 1956 Imperial limousine without the roof (there is no convertible cover). The gunsight-like taillights were an Imperial feature until 1961.

In speed tests and economy runs in 1956, the Imperial tied with the Cadillac for big cars. How many miles per gallon? Fifteen and a half average! That's a 354 V-8 cid with a 5,200-pound car it's hauling around. The Imperial could go from 0 to 60 in 11 seconds, with a top speed of 115. The 354 was a "hemi."

Since the chassis is a 1952 chassis, the car is registered by the city with the state as a 1952 (that is the law in New York). The year of the car goes by the chassis not the body style if the body is changed.

Accessories

Parade Flags
Dual Heaters front and rear
Hand Rails
Leather Interior
Wire Wheels
Foot Rests on Rear Bumper (for security people)
Power Brakes disc on front (the 1952–1955
    Imperials had discs, in 1956 Imperial would
    change over to drum type)
Power Steering
Power Windows
Dual Windshield

1956 *Oldsmobile 88*

The 1956 Olds was just a little different from its predecessor, the 1955. Its grille was more massive looking, built actually as one unit with the bumper.

One of the car's options was a foot button that would change radio stations. Instead of leaning over to change stations (possibly taking your eyes off the road), you simply depressed the foot button and the dial would move until you found the station you wanted and released

Specifications

Factory Price	$2,600	
Overall length	203″	98/212″
Height	60″	
Width	77.6″	
Weight	3,838	3,978
Engine	OHV V-8 324 cid	OHV V-8 324 cid
Bore & Stroke	3⅞ × 3⁷⁄₁₆	same
Compression	9.25:1	same
Horsepower	230 @ 4,400 rpm	240 @ 4,400 rpm
Wheelbase	122″	126″
Suspension	coil front, independent/rear, leaf spring, solid axle	
Fuel tank	20 gals	
Cooling system	21.5 qts	
Tires	7.60 × 15	
Elecrical	12 volts	
Carburetor	2 bbls	4 bbls
Transmission	3-speed manual Hydramatic/optional	

Accessories

Power Steering
Power Brakes
Automatic Transmission
Heater/Defroster
Electric Clock
Six-Way Power Seat
Outside Mirror Driver's Side remote controlled
Power Windows
Air Conditioning
Automatic Headlight Dimmer
Radio with rear speaker and foot control
Rear Window Defogger
Spare Tire
Dual Exhaust
Power Antenna
Windshield Washer
Tinted Glass
Continental Tire (dealer option)
Sun Visor
Spotlight
Padded Instrument Panel
Seat Belts

the button. It may sound gimmicky, but it's really quite a good idea for convenience and safety.

In 1957 Oldsmobile offered a transistorized radio that popped out of the dash to become a portable hand-held unit you could take along with you. The ones being built today can also be popped out, by thieves, not the owner.

1957 *Chevy Bel Air*

"Chevrolet has built tomorrow's car today." That's what some people claimed for the 1957 Chevy. It was the first year for the famed 283 cid V-8, basically the same V-8 that is being used by GM today.

When Rolls Royce went to the V-8 in 1960 it was again based on the same small block as the 283 Chevy. To go along with the 283, Rolls used the Cadillac hydramatic,

Specifications

Factory Price	$2,400	
Overall Length	202.2"	
Height	60.4"	
Width	73.9"	
Weight	2,464	
Engine	OHV V-8	
	283 cid	OHV 6 cyl/235.5 cid
Bore & Stroke	3.87 × 3	3⁹⁄₁₆ × 3¹⁵⁄₁₆
Compression	8.5:1 10.5:1 fuel injection [283 hp @ 6,200 rpm]	8.0:1
Horsepower	185 @ 4,600 rpm	140 @ 4,200 rpm
Wheelbase	115"	
Suspension	coil front, leaf springs rear	
Fuel Tank	20 gals	
Cooling System	17 qts	
Tires	7.50 × 14	
Electrical	12 volts	
Carburetor	2 bbls standard 4 bbls optional fuel injection op Ramjet	
Transmission	3-speed manual with overdrive optional Powerglide/2-speed automatic optional.	

Accessories

Power Steering
Power Brakes
Automatic Transmission
Heater/Defroster
Electric Clock
Six-Way Power Seat
Outside Mirror Driver's Side
Power Windows
Air Conditioning (V-8 only)
Power Trunk
Automatic Headlight Dimmer
Radio with rear speaker, signal seeking
Power Antenna
Rear Window Defogger
Spare Tire
Trip Odometer
Fuel and Temperature Gauges
Seat Belts
Continental Tire
Electric Shaver
Underhood Light

except Rolls tried to improve the hydramatic (they were smart enough to at least let the 283 alone). The owners of early Rollses of the 60s with hydramatics had many problems. But Rolls did not understand the workings of this great automatic and instead of improving it, they ruined it. So much for European engineering.

The big news about Chevy in 1957 was not only the 283 V-8 but also *fuel injection*. With the optional fuel injection, the 283 put out 283 hp or one hp for each cubic inch.

The 1957 Chevy offered several different carburetor set-ups with the 283 engine. In addition to the standard 2 barrel there was the 4 barrel with dual exhaust (Power Pac), dual quads, and fuel injection, the results being:

4 barrel	9.5:1/220 hp @ 4,800 rpm
4 barrel	9.5:1/245 hp @ 5,000 rpm
2 × 4 barrel	9.5:1/270 hp @ 6,000 rpm
fuel inj	10.5:1/283 hp @ 6,200 rpm

1957 Corvette

The racy Corvette is the only real sports car made in the U.S. It first dashed onto the scene in 1954, though actually came out in late 1953. Some people refer to those as 53s but G.M. calls them 54s.

The 1954 Vette had a fiberglass body which it still uses today. The first Vettes were offered only with a straight 6 cylinder engine and automatic transmission and no roll-up windows. Instead plastic curtains were snapped

into place during foul weather. Needless to say, that system didn't work too well.

In 1955 a V-8 was added. Sales were not booming and management thought of doing the car in. But 1955 was also the year of the Thunderbird. For competitive reasons (pride) the Corvette was continued.

The car was restyled slightly in 1956 and also received roll up windows, a manual transmission, and lockable doors. Sales shot up. A removable hardtop was also an option.

Specifications

Factory Price	$3,500	
Overall Length	168"	
Height	51"	
Width	72.8"	
Weight	2,730	
Engine	OHV V-8	
	283 cid	283/optional
Bore & Stroke	3.87 × 3	
Compression	9.5:1	10.5:1
Horsepower	220 @ 4,800 rpm	270 @ 6,000 rpm/dual quads
		283 @ 6,200 rpm/fuel injection
Wheelbase	102"	
Suspension	coil springs front/leaf spring rear, solid axle	
Fuel Tank	16.4 gals	
Cooling System	17 qts	
Tires	6.70 × 15	
Electrical	12 volts	
Carburetor	single 4 bbl	
	dual quads op	
	fuel injection op	
Axle Ratio	3.70:1/4.11:1/4.56:1	
Transmission	3-speed manual standard	
	4-speed optional	
	automatic optional	

Accessories

Radio signal seeking
Heater/Defroster
Power Windows
Detachable Hardtop
Power Top
Windshield Washer
Two-tone Paint
Dual Quads 2 × 4 bbls
Fuel Injection (Ramjet)
Automatic Transmission

By 1957 fuel injection and dual quads (carburetors) were options. The Vette was now truly a performance sports car. It had a top speed of 135 +, went from 0 to 60 mph in 6.1 seconds and covered the ¼ mile in 14.2 seconds. It cost $3,400 and the next closest thing available was a $10,000 European sports car. It was said the "rich bought European sports cars, the wealthy the Vette. They knew value for their dollar."

The 1956/1957 Corvette were almost identical. In 1958 the Vette received quad headlights as its distinguishing feature. It was also advertised with narrow white stripe tires or what are considered contemporary tires today. The Cadillac Eldorado Brougham came with the one inch wide whitewall and it seems some were made for the Vette as an option instead of the wide (2½") whitewall.

In 1959 the Vette would again be advertised with the wide whitewall. In 1962 the Vette went back to the one inch whitewall, as the entire auto industry changed over to the narrow whitewall.

To some people Thunderbird has the magic, to others it's the Vette. If the Vette doesn't stir your imagination or start your blood boiling, donate your organs to a worthy cause, your brain isn't functioning!

1957 *Dodge Royal Hardtop*

In 1957 Chrysler Corporation unveiled its trendy Forward Look. The Dodge of 1957 had style and flair, and just the right amount of chrome without being too heavy. The wing-back design gave it a supercar look—a true 50s Dream Machine.

The 354 cid V-8 was an optional power plant. The heads in the engine were of hemispherical shape—and it

Specifications

Factory Price	$2,700		
Overall Length	212.2″		
Height	54.8″ (sedan 57.3″)		
Width	77.9″		
Weight	3,585		
Luggage Capacity	57.4 cu ft		
Engine	OHV V-8	OHV V-8	L-head in line 6 cyl
	325 cid	354 cid (hemi)	230 cid
Bore & Stroke	3.69 × 3.80	3.94 × 3.63	3.25 × 4.62
Compression	8.5:1	10.0:1	8.0:1
Horsepower	260 @ 4,400	340 @ 5,200	138 @ 4,000
	rpm		285 @ 4,400
			(custom royal)
Wheelbase	122″ (all models)		
Suspension	torsion bar front; semi elliptic rear (leaf springs)		
Fuel Tank	20 gals		
Cooling System	20 qts		
Tires	8.00 × 15		
Electrical	12 volts		
Carburetor	2 bbls	D-500	1 bbl
	4 bbls/op-	dual quads	
	tional	(two 4 bbls)	
Axle Ratio	3.55 automatic/3.7 manual/4.11		
	overdrive		
Transmission	manual standard		
	Powerflite 2-speed automatic		
	(op)		
	Torque-Flite 3-speed automatic		
	(op)		

Accessories

Power Steering
Power Brakes
Automatic Transmission
Heater/Defroster
Electric Clock
Six-Way Power Seat
Outside Mirror Driver's Side remote controlled
Power Windows
Air Conditioning
Radio with rear speaker
Power Antenna
Rear Window Defogger blower type
Power Door Locks
Spare Tire
Trip Odometer
Fuel and Temperature Gauges
Highway Hi-Fi
Seat Belts

98

was the last year Chrysler would use that design. The next year the D-500 option would be a 361 cid V-8 with either dual quads or electronic fuel injection. For the economy minded Dodge also had an in-line 6 cylinder engine displacing 230". It put out 138 hp @ 4,000.

In 1957 Chrysler first used torsion bar suspension in the front. They have used it every year since then. The Chrysler line-up also featured the Highway Hi-Fi, a specially constructed record player that used 7" discs and had a special shock-resistant arm. It worked—but where to store all those Top Tunes of the Fifties?

99

1957 *Pontiac Safari*

The 1955–1957 Safari (and its cousin the Chevy Nomad) seemed more suited to the ever-widening suburbs than to the dusty bush trails of Africa. They were two-door sporty sedans, made to appeal to the new American wanderlust.

The Safari was a bit plusher than the Nomad, leather interior being a standard item. It had some other interesting details too, such as fender ornaments that lit up when the headlights were turned on.

100

Specifications

Factory Price	$3,400	
Overall Length	207.7"/Safari Chieftain	206"/Star Chief
Height	60.1"	
Width	75.2"	213.8"
Weight	3,636	
Engine	OHV V-8 (4 bbls) 347 cid	OHV V-8 (2 bbls) 347 cid 3.94 × 3.56
Bore & Stroke	3.94 × 3.56	
Compression	10.00:1	8.5:1 (Synchromesh) 10.00:1 (Automatic)
Horsepower	270 @ 4,800 rpm	227 @ 4,600 rpm (sync). 252 @ 4,600 rpm (auto.)
Wheelbase	124" (Chieftain 122")	
Suspension	coil springs front, semi-elliptical rear	
Fuel Tank	20 gals	
Cooling System	23.1 qts	
Tires	8.50 × 14	
Electrical	12 volts	
Carburetor*	4 bbls	2 bbls
Transmission	3-speed synchromesh Hydramatic (op.)	

*Pontiac offered a special engine to go along with their "special" car—the Bonneville convertible. It had a tri-power (3 two bbl carb. set up) it used the basic 347 cid engine but with the 3 two's you had
  290 hp @ 5,000 rpm single-breaker point (auto)
  317 hp @ 5,200 rpm dual-breaker point (synch trans)
  317 hp @ 5,200 rpm single-breaker point (auto) with special booster.

Neither the Safari nor the Nomad was a stunning success and both were discontinued after 1957.

Buick and Olds had their counterparts in the Cabellero and Fiesta respectively. They were 4-door hard-top wagons produced in 1957–1958.

Accessories

Power Steering
Power Brakes
Automatic Transmission
Heater/Defroster
Electric Clock
Six-Way Power Seat
Outside Mirror Driver's Side remote controlled
Power Windows
Air Conditioning
Automatic Headlight Dimmer
Radio
Power Antenna
Rear Window Defogger (not on wagon)
Power Door Locks
Spare Tire
Trip Odometer
Fuel and Temperature Gauges
Leather Interior
Seat Belts

1955/56/57 Thunderbird

I n 1955 Ford introduced a hot-shot two-seat sporty car, not exactly a sports car but snazzier than an everyday passenger car. Its name—THUNDERBIRD!

The car was made only for three years as a 2-seater, after that it grew to a 4-seater. The results of those three years are the red (55), white (56), and blue (57) T-Birds seen here.

When I happened to show this picture to a friend who is curator of an art museum, her reply was, "My God,

103

Specifications 1955 *Thunderbird*

Factory Price	$3,000
Overall Length	175.3″
Height	52.2″
Width	70.3″
Weight	2,980
Engine	OHV V-8
	292 cid
Bore & Stroke	3.75 × 3.30
Compression	8.5:1 automatic
	8.1:1 manual and overdrive
Horsepower	198 automatic/190 manual @
	4,400 rpm
Wheelbase	102″
Suspension	independent front/solid rear
	axle
Fuel Tank	17½ gals
Cooling System	21 qts
Tires	6.70 × 15
Electrical	6 volts
Carburetor	single 4 bbl
Axle Ratio	automatic 3.31:1
	manual 3.73:1
	overdrive 3.92:1
Transmission	manual speed
	overdrive
	automatic

Accessories

Power Steering
Power Brakes
Automatic Transmission
Heater/Defroster
Electric Clock
Power Seat four way
Outside Mirror Driver's Side
Power Windows
Radio
Power Antenna
Tilt Wheel
Spare Tire
Trip Odometer
Fuel and Temperature Gauges
Soft Top (on the original 2-seat T-Bird the
    detachable hardtop was standard, the soft top
    was an option)

Specifications 1956 Thunderbird

Factory Price	$3,200	
Overall Length	175.3" (185" including Continental tire)	
Height	52.2"	
Width	70.3"	
Weight	3,088	
Engine	OHV V-8 292 cid	optional V-8 312 cid
Bore & Stroke	3.37 × 3.30	3.80 × 3.44
Compression	3.44:1	3.44:1
Horsepower	200 @ 4,600 rpm	225 @ 4,400 rpm with automatic
Wheelbase	102"	
Suspension	independent front/solid rear axle	
Fuel Tank	17½ gals	
Cooling System	21 qts	
Tires	6.70 × 15	
Electrical	12 volts	
Carburetor	4 bbls	
Axle Ratio	3.78:1 manual 3.89:1 overdrive 3.22:1 automatic	
Transmission	manual 3-speed overdrive Ford-O-Matic	

Accessories

Power Steering
Power Brakes
Automatic Transmission
Heater/Defroster
Electric Clock
Power Seat
Outside Mirror Driver's Side
Power Windows
Radio
Power Antenna
Tilt Wheel
Spare Tire
Trip Odometer
Fuel and Temperature Gauges
Soft Top (hardtop was standard,
    detachable; soft top an option)
Wire Wheels
Chrome Engine Dress-up Kit
Special V-8

Specifications 1957 Thunderbird

Factory Price	$3,400		
Overall Length	181.4"		
Height	51.2"		
Width	70.3"		
Weight	3,134		
Engine*	OHV V-8 312 cid	OHV V-8 312 cid	OHV V-8 312 cid
Bore & Stroke	3.80:1 × 3.44:1	3.80:1 × 3.44:1	3.80:1 × 3.44:1
Compression	9.7:1	10.00:1	8.5:1
Horsepower	245 @ 4,500 rpm	285 @ 5,000 rpm*	300 @ 4,800 rpm
Wheelbase	102		
Suspension	independent front/solid rear axle		
Fuel Tank	17½ gals		
Cooling System	21 qts		
Tires	7.50 × 14		
Electrical	12 volts		
Carburetor	single 4 bbls two 4 bbls 4 bbls with Paxton supercharger		
Axle Ratio	3.10:1 Ford-O-Matic/3.56:1 manual/3.70:1 automatic overdrive		
Transmission	automatic/manual/automatic overdrive		

*The Nascar version of this engine was 340 hp @ 5,300 rpm

Accessories

Power Steering
Power Brakes
Automatic Transmission
Heater/Defroster
Electric Clock
Six-Way Power Seat
Power Windows
Automatic Headlight Dimmer
Radio
Power Antenna
Tilt Wheel
Spare Tire
Trip Odometer
Fuel and Temperature Gauges
Soft Top
Engine Chrome Dress-Up Kit
Special V-8s (there were two: one with two 4 bbls,
    the other with Paxton supercharger)

you mean one person owns all three cars? What's the sense of living any longer, he's reached heaven already."

In 1957 the Bird offered some optional power packages. There was the dual quads, referred to as an E-Bird, and a single four-barrel with supercharger (today known as Turbo) which was referred to as an F-Bird. And the Bird had the guts to back up its sporty looks.

The standard Bird was a hardtop with a removable top to make an open car . . . not a convertible. The convertible top was· an option. But ordering the convertible did not mean the hardtop came automatically with the car. You then had to order the hardtop if you wanted it.

1957 *Lincoln Continental Mark II*

W hat the T-Bird was to the younger and less afflu-ent motorist, the Mark II was to the older, higher-income driver. Its suggested retail price in 1956 was $9,517—$4,000 more than a standard Lincoln, $6,000 more than the two-seat Bird—the only option was air conditioning. A leather interior was not an option. The choice was cloth or leather.

The elegant Mark II was basically a hand-built car with much attention paid to detail. It was extremely well

Specifications

Factory Price	$10,000
Overall Length	218.4"
Height	56.25"
Width	77.5"
Weight	4,825
Engine	OHV V-8
	368 cid
Bore & Stroke	4.0 × 3.66
Compression	10.00:1 (1956 was 9.00:1)
Exhaust System	dual/2 mufflers, 2 resonators
Horsepower	300 @ 4,800 rpm (1956/285 @ 4,000 rpm)
Wheelbase	126"
Suspension	independent front, coil spring/ rear solid axle, semi-elliptic
Fuel Tank	25 gals
Cooling System	25.5 qts
Tires	8.00 × 15
Electrical	12 volts
Frame	perimeter frame/square tube steel, double dropped
Carburetor	4 bbls
Axle Ratio	3.07:1
Transmission	3-speed automatic, torque converter with planetary gears

Accessories

Power Steering
Power Brakes
Automatic Transmission
Heater/Defroster
Electric Clock
Six-Way Power Seat
Outside Mirror Drivers Side
Power Windows
Air Conditioning
Automatic Headlight Dimmer
Radio
Power Antenna
Rear Window Defogger
Power Door Locks
Spare Tire
Trip Odometer
Fuel and Temperature Gauges

constructed and classic in style. The Lincoln used very little chrome, letting the lines of the car speak for themselves.

Two production-line convertibles were made in 1957, and they are still around, one in Massachusetts and one in California, at last count. The sportiness of the T-Bird also reflected style, taste, and elegance. One could buy a T-Bird and have change left over for a four-door Lincoln when a luxury car was needed.

The Mark II was made only in 1956 and 1957. Today, when "personal" and "sporty" cars go for between $20,000 and $40,000, the Mark II would be right at home, and at the top of the heap in style and quality. It was introduced just a little too soon.

When the car left the factory it was wrapped in its own flannel-lined bag . . . not a cover but an actual bag enclosed the entire car . . . not to be opened until reaching the dealer.

1958 *DeSoto Sportsman*

The DeSoto had a flair for the dramatic. Look at that fin! The DeSoto reflected the Forward Look of Chrysler Corporation. Chrysler got the ball rolling with the tail fin craze with their Forward Look in the late 50's.

In 1959 Cadillac would do Chrysler one better with those glorious fins and their bullet-like taillights. (Cadillac introduced the tail fin on their 1948 model and the 1964 Cadillac would be the last car to still sport a tail fin.)

111

The Forward Look was the right expression. In fact they look more futuristic today with their space-ship curves than they did in the pre-moon-rocket days.

Except for the quad headlights in the 1958 model, the 1957 and 1958 were almost identical. In 1957 the quad headlights were an option.

DeSoto would have three more model years. On November 30, 1960, production ceased for DeSoto. From 1928 until model year 1961 (even though production halted in 1960 the last DeSotos were model year 1961), 2,024,629 DeSotos were built. They were good cars, but never quite that popular as a division for Chrysler to keep producing.

Specifications

Factory price	$3,700
Overall length	218.6" (Fireflite)
	216.5" Firesweep
	220" Wagon
Height	55.1" (other models from 56" to 57")
Width	78.3"
Weight	3,930 (3,660 to 4,000)
Engine	OHV V-8/350 cid
	OHV V-8/361 cid
Bore & Stroke	4.06 × 3.38
	4.12 × 3.38
Compression	10.00:1
	10.25:1
Carburetor	2 bbls
	4 bbls (op)
	dual quads (op)
Horsepower	280 @ 4,600 rpm 2 bbls 350 cid
	295 @ 4,600 rpm 2 bbls 361 cid
	305 @ 4,600 rpm 4 bbls 361 cid
	345 @ 5,000 rpm two 4 bbls (dual quads) 361 cid
Wheelbase	126" (Firesweep 122")
Suspension	
Torsion bar front/semi-elliptic rear	
Fuel Tank	20 gals
Cooling Systems	23 qts
Tires	8.50 × 14
Electrical	12 volts
Transmission	manual 3-speed
	Powerflite (2-speed automatic)
	Torque-Flite (3-speed automatic)

De Soto had four models: Fireseep/Firedome/Fireflite/Adventurer

Accessories

Power Steering
Power Brakes
Automatic Transmission
Heater/Defroster
Electric Clock
Six-Way Power Seat
Outside Mirror Driver's Side remote controlled
Power Windows
Air Conditioning
Automatic Headlight Dimmer
Radio
Power Antenna
Rear Window Defogger
Power Door Locks
Spare Tire
Trip Odometer
Fuel and Temperature Gauges
Seat Belts
Highway Hi-Fi Automatic Record Player

1958 *Cadillac Sedan De Ville*

P robably no car has ever represented the American Dream as perfectly as the Cadillac Sedan De Ville. "I've arrived," it said. "I made it and I'm glad."

In 1958 Cadillac offered two versions of the car, one ten inches longer than the other, called the extended deck. Guess which one was the favorite? A smaller Cadillac, not in 1958!

That year marked an end of an era for Cadillac. The famed Dagmars, the hidden gas cap in the taillight on the drivers side, even the gold V and crest were to disappear. From 1959 stainless steel would replace the gold V. The other items would appear no more.

It was also the last year of the postwar car, even though it did not look that way. The 58s were still a "tall" car. In 1959 they would be lower by three to five inches depending on the model. They would remain there until today. Almost all the options available today were already present in 1958, except for some electronic wizardry.

Specifications

Factory price	$5,400
Overall length	225.3" (short deck 216.8")
Height	59.1"
Width	80"
Weight	4,930
Engine	OHV V-8
	365 cid
Bore & Stroke	4 × 3.62
Compression	10.25:1
Horsepower	310 @ 4,800 rpm
Wheelbase	129.5" (series 60 133")
Suspension	coil springs front and rear
Fuel Tank	20 gals
Cooling System	18.7 qts
Tires	8.20 × 15
Electrical	12 volts
Frame	X-frame
Carburetor	single 4 bbls
Axle Ratio	3.07:1 (3.07:1 op)
Transmission	Hydramatic (4-speed automatic)

Accessories

Power Steering
Power Brakes
Automatic Transmission
Heater/Defroster ducts for rear
Electric Clock
Six-Way Power Seat
Outside Mirror Driver's Side remote controlled
Power Windows power vent optional
Air Conditioning ducts for rear
Power Trunk
Cruise Control
Automatic Headlight Dimmer
Radio with rear speaker, signal seeking
Power Antenna
Rear Window Defogger
Power Door Locks
Spare Tire
Trip Odometer
Fuel and Temperature Gauges
Window Lock Switch

It was also the last year the chrome was nickel plated. The 1958 Cadillac was on the apex of an era that represented the American car, the Dream Machine!

1958 *Eldorado Brougham*

J ust as Ford decided to stop producing its Mark II, Cadillac brought out its Eldorado Brougham. The car listed at $13,074, more than even a Rolls Royce of that period.

The Eldorado had just about everything and anything one could want on a car (then or now). The only difference between the 1957 model and the 1958 was under the hood. The 1957 version had dual quads, while in 1958 tri-power was the set-up.

Among the many items that were standard on the car (there were no options, only choices . . . color, fabric or

Specifications

Factory price	$13,074
Overall length	216.3"
Height	55.5"
Width	78.5"
Weight	5,315
Engine	OHV V-8
	365 cid
Bore & Stroke	4 × 3.62
Compression	10.25:1
Horsepower	335 @ 4,800 rpm
Wheelbase	125"
Suspension	air suspension/rubber air bags
	pressurized by small compressor
Fuel Tank	20 gals
Cooling System	22.6 qts
Tires*	8.20 × 15
Electrical	12 volts
Frame	X-frame
Carburetor	tri-power (three dual carbs)
	1957 dual quads (two 4 bbls)
Axle Ratio	3.36:1 (3.77:1 op)
Transmission	Hydramatic (4-speed automatic)

*The 1957–58 Eldorado Brougham was the first car (until 1961) to offer the so-called "modern day whitewall," 1" wide as opposed to the "wider" whitewall of 2¼" that started from the hubcap out 2¼". Some cars were 3". The wide whitewall was getting narrower slightly from 1949 (5") until the 2¼" of 1958–1961 vintage was reached. Then the one inch to 1½". white stripe width look took over.

**The 1958 Corvette also offered a 1" stripe whitewall.

leather interior) was the memory seat. You could set the power front seat to different positions, for two different drivers. In addition the seat was the normal six-way power seat. When the car was started, the antenna would automatically rise, when the radio or car motor was turned off the antenna would automatically lower (in addition to being the standard power antenna). If the car was going more than five mph the doors would automatically lock. If the door was not fully closed, the car would not move from a dead start. With a roof of brushed stainless steel, the car stood a low 55.5", which was quite revolutionary for a four-door car then. Standard were one-inch whitewalls, an industry first, which would not appear again until 1962.

Air suspension was standard. Small rubber bags, replacing the standard springs, pressurized by a small compressor (powered by its own electric motor), regulated the car's ride and height.

In theory the air suspension sounded great. In practice it did nothing very different from the standard suspension except for losing pressure after sitting for a few days.

The result would be a dead-looking Brougham. The car would be sitting almost on the ground. After running for about fifteen minutes enough pressure was worked up to pump air back into the bags and raise the car up to its normal driving height. The problem with the air suspension was more of non-use than abuse. I know of one Eldorado that is still in daily use in northern New Jersey and still has the air bag suspension with never any problems.

Another feature the car had: when either rear door was opened the front seat automatically moved forward, and then returned to its normal position after the door was closed.

Take a good look at those massive Dagmars. 1958

Accessories

Power Steering
Power Brakes
Automatic Transmission
Heater/Defroster
Electric Clock
Six-Way Power Seat (memory seat)
Outside Mirror Drivers' Side remote controlled
Power Windows
Air Conditioning
Power Trunk
Cruise Control
Automatic Headlight Dimmer
Radio
Power Antenna
Twilight Sentinel
Rear Window Defogger
Power Door Locks
Automatic Parking Brake Release
Spare Tire
Trip Odometer
Fuel and Temperature Gauges
Window Lock Switch
Personalized Notepad and Pencil
Tissue Dispenser/Perfume Dispenser
Glovebox Vanity
Brushed Stainless Steel Roof

was the last year Cadillac would use the projectile-type bumper. It would also be the last year for the gas cap to be hidden under the driver's side taillight.

The Brougham would continue for two more years, but the body would be made in Italy by Pininfarina. They were longer than the downsized 1957/58 Detroit Broughams and after the 1960 model year were quietly put to rest.

The 1957/58 Broughams had center opening doors, something that the 1959/60 version did not. Lincoln would pick this 30s design theme up in 1961 and use it on their models through 1969.

1958 *Cadillac Eldorado Biarritz*

The 1958 Biarritz was the last year that the Eldorado would be a separate bodied car from the rest of the Cadillac line-up. Not until the front-wheel drive Eldorados of 1967 would the Eldorado be different from other Cadillac's.

In hardtop form the 1958 Eldorado was known as the Seville. It was not a front-wheel drive car of four doors that came in the 80s. Originally the Eldorado Seville was a two-door hardtop.

Specifications

Factory Price	$8,300
Overall Length	223.4"
Height	58"
Width	80"
Weight	5,100
Engine	OHV V-8
	365 cid
Bore & Stroke	4 × 3.62
Compression	10.25:1
Horsepower	335 @ 4,800 rpm
Wheelbase	129.5"
Suspension	coil springs front and rear
Fuel Tank	20 gals
Cooling System	18.7 qts
Tires	8.20 × 15
Electrical	12 volts
Carburetor	3 dual barrels/tri-power
Axle Ratio	3.77:1
Transmission	Hydramatic
Frame	X-frame

Accessories

Power Steering
Power Brakes
Automatic Transmission
Heater/Defroster
Electric Clock
Six-Way Power Seat
Outside Mirror Driver's Side remote controlled
Power Windows including Vent
Air Conditioning
Power Trunk
Cruise Control
Automatic Headlight Dimmer
Radio
Power Antenna
Rear Window Defogger
Power Door Locks
Spare Tire
Trip Odometer
Fuel and Temperature Gauges
Window Lock Switch
Air Suspension

The Eldorado was different from the standard Caddy not only in looks but also mechanics. It came with tri-power (3 dual-barrel carbs.) instead of the standard single 4 barrel as in other Cadillacs.

The Eldorados were also slightly ahead of Cadillacs in styling trends. The fin on the 1958 was not as pronounced as the regular Cadillac line-up. In 1959 and 1960 the Cadillac fin would grow to its greatest height. By comparison the 1958 Eldorado is rather sedate.

The only difference between the 1958 and 1957 Eldorado's besides some chrome trim was the headlights. The 1957 model had single headlights and in 1958 Caddy (as all cars) went to quad headlights (4). In 1958 the Eldorado had tri-power and in 1957 it used 2 four barrels.

The Eldorados were fully optioned cars. The only extra was air conditioning. The wheels on the Eldorado were called Sabre wheels. They were aluminum and just the emblem cap popped off. In 1958 money the wheels cost about $200 each!

1958 *Pontiac Bonneville*

The Pontiac Bonneville was not designed for super-marketing. Its optional bucket seats attracted those who wanted a stylish, action-oriented car that rode like a luxury model, a sporty car with boulevard comfort and manners. If you wanted performance, it was there.

In 1958 the Bonneville came in two models, hard-top and convertible. The year before it had been available only in a convertible (with fuel injection).

The 1958 model offered either four-barrel car-

Specifications

Factory Price	$3,500	
Overall Length	210.5″ (Chieftain, also Star Chief 215″)	
Height	55.6″ (all others 57″)	
Width	77.4″	
Weight	3,825	
Engine	OHV V-8	OHV V-8 (optional)
	370 cid	370 cid
Bore & Stroke	4.06 × 3.56	same
Compression	10.5:1	same
*Horsepower	300 @ 4,600 rpm	
	tri-power	310 @ 4,800
Wheelbase	122″/Chieftain 122″	Star Chief 124″
Suspension	coil front, coil rear/(air suspension optional)	
Fuel Tank	20 gals	
Cooling System	22.3 qts	
Tires	8.00 × 14	
Electrical	12 volts	
Frame	X-frame	
Carburetor	3 dual-bbl carbs	fuel injection
Transmission	3-speed Synchromesh standard	
	4-speed Hydramatic optional	

*The base Pontiac engine was the 370 cid with either 2 bbls or 4 bbls

buretor, tri-power or fuel injection. Air suspension was an option most people, fortunately, did not opt for.

The Bonneville also featured the Sportable radio. It slid into the dash and plugged into the car's power system and speakers. When removed from the car it became a battery-operated transistor radio with built-in speaker and its own leather carrying case.

A white tri-powered Bonneville convertible was chosen as the pace car for the Indy 500 that year.

Accessories

Power Steering
Power Brakes
Automatic Transmission
Heater/Defroster
Electric Clock
Six-Way Power Seat
Outside Mirror Driver's Side remote controlled
Power Windows
Air Conditioning
Power Trunk
Cruise Control
Automatic Headlight Dimmer
Radio
Power Antenna
Rear Window Defogger
Power Door Locks
Spare Tire
Trip Odometer
Fuel and Temperature Gauges
Window Lock Switch
Individual Bucket Seat front and rear
Air Suspension
Fuel Injection
Tri-Power 3 dual-bbl carburetors

1959 *Edsel*

The name Edsel is as famous as that of Mustang and Thunderbird in the Ford roster, but for entirely opposite reasons. Edsel is now a much used word in the American vocabulary—to signify a blunder of epic proportions. For that's what the Edsel was.

This is not to say that the car was a lemon. Indeed it wasn't. It just came out at the wrong time. Despite years of marketing research (so much for marketing research) and lots of investment money, the Edsel could not com-

pete with the economic problems of the recession years of 1957 through 1961.

It was radical in design, with a horse-collar grille that reminded some people of a part of the human anatomy, and its back view was far from the usual. Had the

128

Specifications

Factory Price	$3,100		
Overall Length	211″		
Height	56″		
Width	80″		
Weight	3,790		
*Engine	**OHV V-8	OHV V-8	OHV 6 cyl
	332 cid	292 cid	223 cid
Bore & Stroke	4 × 3.30	3.75 × 3.30	3.62 × 3.60
Compression	8.9:1	8.8:1	8.4:1
Horsepower	225 @ 4,000 rpm	200 @ 4,400 rpm	145 @ 4,000 rpm
Wheelbase	120		
Fuel Tank	20 gals		
Cooling System	20 qts		
Tires	7.50 × 14		
Electrical	12 volts		
Carburetor	4 bbl	2 bbl	1 bbl
Axle Ratio	332 cid/V-8	292 cid/V-8	223 cid/6 cyl
	3.56:1 manual	3.56:1 manual	3.70:1 manual
	2.91:1 Ford-O-Matic	2.91:1 Ford-O-Matic	3.56:1 Ford-O-Matic
	2.69:1 Cruise-O-Matic		
Transmission	manual (overdrive op)		
	Ford-O-Matic		
	Cruise-O-Matic		

*The 332 V-8 was the standard engine in the Corsair series.

**There was an optional 361 OHV V-8 that was optional on all series. This was a 4-bbl carb. engine with:
9.6:1 comp.
4.05 × 3.50 bore & stroke
303 hp @ 4,600 rpm

Accessories

Power Steering
Power Brakes
Automatic Transmission
Heater/Defroster
Electric Clock
Six-Way Power Seat
Outside Mirror Driver's Side remote controlled
Power Windows
Air Conditioning
Power Trunk
Cruise Control
Radio
Power Antenna
Rear Window Defogger
Power Door Locks
Spare Tire
Trip Odometer
Fuel and Temperature Gauges
Seat Belts
Spotlight passenger's and driver's side

times been more optimistic, the car might have made it. But when people feel economically insecure they don't want to adjust to a flamboyant total new look.

The car was named for Edsel Ford, son of the first Henry Ford. (Henry Ford II is Edsel's son.) Edsel was not cut out for the automobile business, and his father was a tyrant in the industry. Edsel couldn't make it with a boss like that who was also his father, and he developed ulcers and finally cancer. He died in 1943, at age fifty. Apparently his son Henry never wanted the project to be called Edsel, perhaps fearing it too would be doomed. But the name prevailed and the car didn't.

It was a time when people were bucking the Detroit chromes and looking for a transportation car that was cheap and inexpensive to operate. At that time such cars were called compacts (though some of the early compacts would be considered full size by today's standards). The Rambler, made by American Motors, filled the bill.

129

There were numerous European makes, but many seemed too small and too cheap. (Ever try to get into a Fiat/Seat? . . . that was the name of the model.) There was one company, though, that made a funny-looking car (shades of the 1935 DeSoto Airflow) and made it well, with room for four people. The name was VOLKSWAGEN!

The Edsel was made model years 1958, 1959, and 1960. In 1958 Edsel sold 33,800; in 1959, 44,700; and in 1960, when the word was out that the car was to be no longer, 2,946.

1959 *Ford Skyliner*

T ry to imagine a hardtop (steel or some metal-type roof) that could transform itself into a convertible. The metal top would fold in a few places, the trunk would open automatically (the lid moving backwards toward the bumper) and the entire top would then lower itself into the trunk, which would then lower its lid, and there would be one clean sweep of fender. Seems like a fantasy? Ford made such a vehicle from 1957 to 1959.

It was not a show car or prototype but an everyday

Specifications

Factory Price	$3,400
Overall Length	208.1″
Height	56.2″
Width	78″
Weight	4,000
Engine	OHV V-8 292 cid
Bore & Stroke	3.75 × 3.30
Compression	8.8:1
Horsepower	200 @ 4,400 rpm
Wheelbase	118″
Suspension	coil front, independent/leaf springs rear, solid axle
Fuel Tank	20 gals
Cooling System	20 qts
Tires	8.00 × 14
Electrical	12 volts
Carburetor	2 bbls
Transmission	3-speed manual overdrive/optional Ford-O-Matic/optional Cruise-O-Matic/optional

Accessories

Power Steering
Power Brakes
Automatic Transmission
Heater/Defroster
Electric Clock
Six-Way Power Seat
Outside Mirror Driver's Side remote controlled
Power Windows
Air Conditioning
Cruise Control
Radio
Power Antenna
Rear Window Defogger
Power Door Locks
Spare Tire
Trip Odometer
Fuel and Temperature Gauges
Seat Belts
Air Suspension

production car called the Skyliner. It was an engineering marvel, and it worked! The mechanism was trouble-free. But sales were not as expected and after model year 1959 the car was discontinued. The same basic mechanism was used on the soft top T-Bird convertible through 1966.

The Skyliner sold 20,766 in 1957; in 1958, 14,713 were sold; and the final year, 1959, 12,915. To American car manufacturers these numbers represented a product the public did not accept. Ford dropped the car. In each of those years Ford sold three times as many Sunliner convertibles (the conventional soft top) as the Skyliner.

The car was a success in that it worked and a number of people bought it, but not enough to satisfy Ford.

1959 *Oldsmobile 98*

Take a look at the pancake roof with almost 360 degrees of visibility. This roof line would appear for two years, 1959 and 1960, and then disappear. The 1959 Olds was a much cleaned up car as compared to the 1958. Gobs of the chrome that people either hated or loved on the 1958 was gone on the 1959 model (yes, this is a toned-down car!).

The car was a work of mobile sculpture. The taillight is suitable for framing by itself. When you sat behind the wheel of this beauty there was no craning the neck to look out or moving your head from side to side because the slope of the windshield, combined with the size of the

134

rear-view mirror, makes it almost impossible to see. The windows in the rear doors went down . . . all the way (electrically) for an open-air kind of ride in your own scenic cruiser. If you cruised too fast a buzzer warned you when you exceeded the preset speed of the cruise control. The era of talking cars was beginning.

Specifications

Factory Price	$4,300	
Overall Length	223" (88 series 218")	
Height	54"	
Width	81"	
Weight	4,698	
Engine		Dynamic 88 OHV V-8
	OHV V-8	OHV V-8
	394 cid	371 cid
Bore & Stroke	4.13 × 3.69	4. × 3.69
Compression	9.75:1	9.75:1
Horsepower	315 @ 4,600 rpm	270 @ 4,600 rpm
Wheelbase	26"	123"
Suspension	coil springs front and rear	
Fuel Tank	21 gals	
Cooling System	21 qts	
Tires	9.00 × 14	
Electrical	12 volts	
Frame	tubular X	
Carburetor	4 bbls	2 bbls (4 op)
Axle Ratio	3.42:1	3.07:1
Transmission	Hydramatic	

Accessories

Power Steering
Power Brakes
Automatic Transmission/Cruise Control
Heater/Defroster
Electric Clock
Six-Way Power Seat
Outside Mirror Driver's Side remote controlled
Power Windows including vent/Window Lock Switch
Air Conditioning
Power Trunk
Automatic Headlight Dimmer
Radio rear speaker, signal seeking, floor switch
Power Antenna
Rear Window Defogger
Power Door Locks
Spare Tire
Trip Odometer
Fuel and Temperature Gauges
Seat Belts
E-Z-Eye Glass
Air Suspension

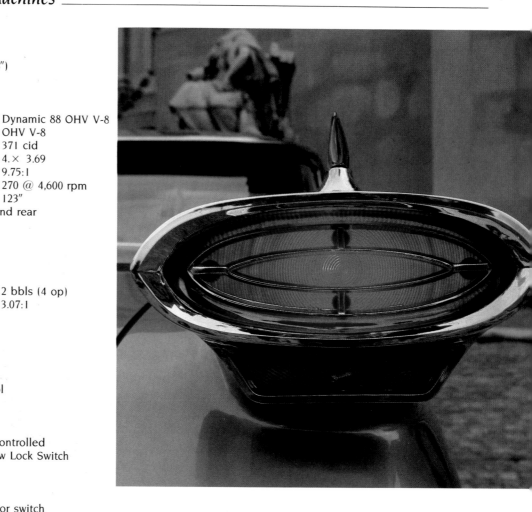

1959/60 Cadillac/Fleetwood 60/75

C adillac introduced the fin in 1948. It was nothing more than a gentle sloping upward of the rear fender in which the taillight rested. In 1957 Chrysler Corporation came out with their "Forward Look," in which their entire line-up sported big graceful fins.

It seems Cadillac could not let anyone upstage them and the result is the 1959 models seen here. But the fin alone does not distinguish this car. It is also the shape of the fin and those two bulletlike taillights that protrude on each fin. The car had rocketship styling, it was big and it was powerful. The Eldorado came with tri-power and combined with that 390 V-8 and 4-speed hydramatic this car had the guts to go with its rocket ship look. This is a 5,200-

Specifications

Factory Price	$ 7,000 (Fleetwood 60)
	$10,000 (Limousine)
Overall Length	225" (Limousine 244.8")
Overall Height	
6-window sedan	56.2"/Fleetwood 60 Special
4-window sedan	54.3"
2-door hardtop	54.1"
convertible	54.2"
Biarritz	54.9"
Seville	54.8"
Limousine	59.3"
Width	80.1"
Weight	5,100/Fleetwood 60
	5,600/Limousine
Engine	OHV V-8
	390 cid
Bore & Stroke	4 × 3.87
Compression	10.5:1
Horsepower	325 @ 4,800 rpm
Wheelbase	130" (Limousine 149.5")
Suspension	coil springs all four wheel
	air suspension/optional
Cooling System	19.25 qts
Carburetor	4 bbl
	Eldorado tri-power 345 hp @
	4,800 rpm
Tires	8.20 × 15
Transmission	Hydramatic/4-speed automatic
Fuel Tank	20 gals
Electrical	12 volts
Frame	X-frame

pound car that can go from 0 to 60 in 10 seconds and have a top speed that was more than double the national limit of 55.

In addition to its rocketship look, the car was well made. A TANK, as many owners agree. The ride and quality of the car are truly "The Standard of the World." The conveniences that were available on the car ranged from power windows, door locks, power trunk with pull down, automatic headlight dimmer, cruise control, fog lights, air conditioning. Everything but an FM radio. The car was REAL IRON!

In Limousine form the Cadillac is referred to as the series 75. It was not a chopped and extended version of a smaller car. It was a 2,44.8" car that was built on its own chassis. Its height of 59.3" makes entering and exiting easy. The long graceful lines which culminate in those spectacular (or ridiculous) fins with their bullet lights give the car a formal yet youthful look. The car is only two inches less in height than a Rolls but does not look as cumbersome.

The car came with wool broadcloth in the rear (pas-

senger) compartment and leather in front. The air conditioning was separate for driver and passenger, same with the heating. Power door locks, air suspension, all the accessories available on Cadillac then were also standard. The rear doors on the limousine had lights on the bottom of the door to light up the ground at night to show the way into the car. This was a 5,600-pound-plus living room on wheels.

The 1959/60 Cadillacs were an illusion, a designer's sleight of hand. For all its appearance of great length (not that they are small), the car is only three inches longer

Accessories

Power Steering
Power Brakes self adjusting (1960)
Automatic Transmission
Heater/Defroster
Electric Clock
Six-Way Power Seat
Outside Mirror Driver's Side remote controlled
Power Vent Windows
Air Conditioning
Power Trunk
Cruise Control
Automatic Headlight Dimmer
Radio
Power Antenna
Rear Window Defogger
Power Door Locks
Automatic relase for emergency brake (1960) when
    car is shifted into gear, break releases
    automatically.
Spare Tire
Trip Odometer
Fuel and Temperature Gauges
Window Lock Switch with cars equipped with power
    windows, enables one to raise or lower
    windows without turning on engine.
Air Suspension
Bucket Seats
Fog Lights

than a 1984 Cadillac. Actually the longest Caddys made (and Lincolns) were in the early 70s. The 1979 Lincoln is 231″ long, six more than the 1959/60 Caddy. The Caddys of 1973–1976 were 227″ and 231″ for the Fleetwood.

The 1960 Cadillac is basically a cleaned-up version of the 1959 body style. There is less chrome and the fin appears to be lower. The fin is only one inch lower than the 1959 but the absence of the bullet lights and the sweep of the rear fender that gives the illusion of the 1959 being much higher. The rear chrome taillight housing on the 1959 is lower than on the 1960 and the fin sweeps upward from this housing. On the 1960 model the taillight is in the housing and in the fin but it starts to sweep upward a few inches before the chrome housing.

Of the two fins the 1960 is the more dangerous. It has a sharper point and no bullet lights extending out from the fin to soften (and warn of impaling) the blow.

Among the safety features on the 1960 Caddy are a self-releasing emergency brake. When the car is engaged in either forward or reverse, the emergency brake is automatically disengaged.

This also enables the emergency brake to act as a true auxilliary or back-up system if the power brake system fail. The emergency brake can never "lock" while the car is in gear. It acts like a normal braking system.

The 60 Special is distinguished by its handfitted, weather-resistant fabric roof in perfectly matched body color.

When talking about fins the 1959 and 1960 Caddies are mentioned as being one unit, so close are they in looks and popularity. The term BATMOBILE almost invariably refers to these two model years of cars.

There are certain words or phrases that conjure up something in a person's mind. Say PINK CADILLAC CONVERTIBLE, you said it all.

1960 *Imperial LeBaron*

From its formal stainless-steel-lined roof to its dual air conditioning (one unit for the front, under the hood, the other in the trunk for the rear) to its optional swivel seats, the Imperial says elegance and luxury.

The swivel seat (front only) swings out automatically when the door is opened. The dash panel is lighted electro-luminescently, that is, there are no lamp bulbs. The panel instruments light up with a phosphorescent glow

142

Specifications

Factory Price	$7,100
Overall Length	226.3″
Height	56.7″
Width	80.1″
Weight	4,960
Engine	OHV V-8
	413 cid
Bore & Stroke	4.18 × 3.75
Compression	10.00:1
Horsepower	350 @ 4,600 rpm
Wheelbase	129″
Suspension	torsion bar front/leaf springs rear
Fuel Tank	23 gals
Cooling System	25 qts
Tires	8.90 × 14
Electrical	12 volts
Carburetor	single 4 bbls
Transmission	automatic (Torqueflite)

Luggage Capacity   For comparison with new cars (especially so-called liftbacks with extra cargo space), the trunk of the Le Baron can hold 59.5 cubic feet of cargo . . . with six people in the car and the luggage compartment closed to the world!

Accessories

Power Steering/Power Brakes
Automatic Transmission
Heater/Defroster
Electric Clock
Six-Way Power Seat
Outside Mirror Driver's Side remote controlled
Power Windows including vent windows
Air Conditioning
Power Trunk
Cruise Control
Automatic Headlight Dimmer
Radio/Power Antenna
Rear Window Defogger
Power Door Locks
Spare Tire
Trip Odometer
Fuel and Temperature Gauges
Window Lock Switch
Swivel Seat front seat swivels 45° for ease of entry
    when front door is opened (automatically)

that is glare free and shadowless. It is the best designed dash panel ever seen and the easiest on the eyes, especially on long trips.

The strength of these Imperials (1957–1966) is known widely at demolition derbies. The derbies are so destructive that in some places they are outlawed. The Imperials have proved indestructible. About the only thing that can knock one out of commission is another Imperial.

1960 *Lincoln*

T he 1960 Lincoln was little changed from the 1958 or 1959. But 1961 would mark a big changeover for Lincoln with their center opening rear door. In 1960 Lincoln went back to leaf springs from the coils spring rear suspension they used in 1958 and 1959.

The Continental was a little fancier version of the Lincoln, noted especially for its inward-slanting rear window that went up and down from a switch the driver controlled. The Mark V convertible had a full-width glass win-

145

Specifications

Factory Price	$5,500
Overall Length	227"
Height	56.5"
Width	80.1"
Weight	5,000
Engine	OHV V-8
	430 cid
Bore & Stroke	4.30 × 3.75
Compression	10.5:1
Horsepower	315 @ 4,100 rpm
Wheelbase	131"
Suspension	coil front, semi-elliptic rear
Fuel Tank	22 gals
Cooling System	23 qts
Tires	9.50 × 14
Electrical	12 volts
Frame	unitbody
Carburetor	2 bbls
Axle Ratio	2.87:1 (3.07:1 op)
Transmission	Turbo-drive automatic

Accessories

Power Steering
Power Brakes
Automatic Transmission
Heater/Defroster
Electric Clock
Six-Way Power Seat
Outside Mirror Driver's Side remote controlled
Power Windows including vent windows
Air Conditioning
Power Trunk
Cruise Control
Automatic Headlight Dimmer
Radio with FM converter
Power Antenna
Rear Window Defogger
Power Door Locks
Spare Tire
Trip Odometer
Fuel and Temperature Gauges
Window Lock Switch

dow that went up and down and was completely hidden when the top was lowered. It was quite a car.

There is virtually no item available today that was not available on the 1960 Lincoln. There was even a factory FM converter for your listening pleasure.

Lincoln was still trying to be an "economy" car, if there is such a thing for a big car. It had a two-barrel carburetor which it would continue to use until 1962, finally realizing all it did was give the car less punch with no improvement in economy.

The 1958–1960 Lincolns were the biggest unit cars ever made.

1960 *Nash Metropolitan*

W hen economy and space were called for, Nash answered with this smugly attractive compact Metropolitan. But the cry was not yet loud enough and the car, though fun to drive and simple to maintain, was doomed to failure, even the convertible model.

It had an overall length of just 12½ feet, a small 1.5 (90.9 cid) engine, unit body, and 40 mpg.

The Met was made from 1954 until 1963, designed by Nash and built by Austin of England. The price in 1961 money . . . $1,700.

148

Specifications

Factory Price	$1,700
Overall Length	150″
Height	55″
Width	62″
Weight	1,835
Engine	OHV 4 cyl
	90.89 cid (1.5 liter)
Bore & Stroke	2.88 × 3.50
Compression	8.3:1
Horsepower	55 @ 4,500 rpm
Wheelbase	85″
Suspension	coil front/leaf-spring rear, solid axle
Fuel Tank	10.5 gals
Cooling System	8 qts
Tires	5.20 × 13
Electrical	12 volts
Frame	unit body
Carburetor	1 bbl
Transmission	manual/3-speed

Accessories

Radio
Heater/Defroster
Whitewall Tires

149

1960 *Plymouth Fury*

The 1960 Plymouth spelled the end of the Forward Look for Chrysler. Next year, the car would boast no fins. It would not have the wedge look . . . low in front, high in rear.

The Fury was a new fun car to drive. "Don't you just want to go for a ride?" it seemed to say. It was easy and friendly to have around.

The Plymouth Fury had an optional item called Ram Induction, which in effect was a supercharger. This was available on the Golden Commando, or Sonoramic Commando V-8, the more technical term.

150

Specifications

Factory Price	$3,000		
Overall Length	209.4″		
Height	54.6″		
Width	78.6″		
Weight	3,630		
Engine	OHV V-8	OHV V-8 (Golden Commando)	OHV 6 cyl
	318 cid	361 cid	225.5 cid
Compression	9:1	10:1	8.5:1
Bore & Stroke	3.91 × 3.37/4.12 × 3.38	3.40 × 4.12	
Horsepower	230 @ 4,400 rpm	304 @ 4,600 rpm	145 @ 4,000 rpm
Wheelbase	118″		
Suspension	torsion bar front/leaf-spring rear		
Fuel Tank	20 gals		
Cooling System	21 qts		
Tires	7.50 × 14		
Electrical	12 volts		
Frame	unitbody		
Carburetor	2 bbls	4 bbls	2 bbls
Transmission	manual/3-speed		
	Torqueflite/automatic optional		

Accessories

Power Steering
Power Brakes
Automatic Transmssion
Heater/Defroster
Electric Clock
Six-Way Power Seat
Outside Mirror Driver's Side
  remote controlled
Power Windows
Air Conditioning
Power Trunk
Cruise Control
Automatic Headlight Dimmer
Radio with RCA automatic
  record player
Power Antenna
Power Door Locks
Spare Tire
Trip Odometer
Fuel and Temperature Gauges
Power Swivel Seat

1960 *Rambler*

R eady for any lifestyle was this Rambler—a honey of a car. It was a great car for traveling, with reclining front seats with headrests—the seats would even flatten into a bed.

The Rambler was a unit body car that got between 18 and 29 miles per gallon depending on the engine and carburetor set-up.

Since specifications can say more than just words, following the Rambler specs, there will be the specs for the

152

new breed of GM cars, Cadillac in particular, model year 1985. Remember the Rambler was considered a "compact" car in its time.

In 1962 the Rambler would go to the dual braking system, one cylinder for the front, one for the rear. In case of failure in one cylinder there were brakes to stop the car. In a few years this system would be required by law, and the lowly Rambler had it back then, with seat belts and headrests, mind you.

Specifications 1960 Rambler

Factory Price	$2,200		
Overall Length	189.5″	198.5″ Ambassador	
Height	57.25″	Rebel V-8	
Width	72.25″		
Weight	2,950	3,290	3,400
Engine	OHV 6 cyl	OHV V-8	OHV V-8
	195.6 cid	250 cid	327 cid
Bore & Stroke	3.12 × 4.2	3.5 × 3.25	4 × 3.25
Compression	8.7:1	8.7:1	8.7:1
Horsepower	127 @ 4,200 rpm	200 @ 4,900 rpm	250 @ 4,700
Wheelbase	108″		117″
Suspension	coil springs front & rear		
Fuel Tank	20 gals		
Cooling System	11 qts	21 qts	
Tires	6.40 × 15	7.50 × 14	
Electrical	12 volts		
Frame	unitbody		
Carburetor	1 bbl	2 bbls	4 bbls
		(4 bbls op)	
Transmission	manual/3-speed		
	overdrive optional		
	automatic optional		

*optional dual exhaust boosts hp to 270.

Specifications 1985 Cadillac

Factory Price	$20,000
Overall Length	195″
Height	55″
Width	71.7″
Weight	3,273 coupe
	3,340 sedan
	3,364 Fleetwood
Engine	OHV V-8
	249.7 cid (4.1 liter)
Compression	9.0:1
Wheelbase	110.8″
Suspension	independent
Fuel Tank	18 gals
Tires	P205 × 14 (7.50 × 14)
Electrical	12 volts
Frame	unitbody
Carburetor	fuel injection
Axle Ratio	2.97:1
Transmission	automatic with overdrive
Tread	front 60.3″
	rear 59.8″
Brakes	hydraulic, dual master cylinder

Accessories 1960 *Rambler*

Power Steering
Power Brakes
Power Windows
Seat Belts
Airliner Type Reclining Seat
Individual Front Seats
Automatic Transmission
Heater/Defroster Weather Eye*
Air Conditioning
Overdrive Transmission
E-Stick
Power-Saver-Fan
Twin-Grip Differential
Headrests
Radio
Electric Clock
Safety Plate Glass
Tinted Glass
Spare Tire
Parking Brake Warning Light
Power Door Locks
Air Suspension
Rear Window Defogger
Cruise Control

*"Weather Eye" refers to the Nash heater of 1937. Until then the hot air was recirculated over and over. Nash was the first manufacturer to introduce the modern heating/ventilation system in a car. It brought fresh air in with the heat. The name "Weather Eye" has been used since.

Accessories 1985 *Cadillac*

Power Windows
Power Steering
Power Brakes (dual system)
Electronic Level Control
Front Wheel Drive
Parking Brake release automatic
Spare Tire, Compact type
Transmission 4-speed automatic with overdrive
Recliner, Manual driver's and passenger side
  (optional)
Split Seat (optional)
Trunk Lid Release power and pull down
Electronic Climate Control heater, defroster, air
  conditioning
Unit Body
Door Locks electrically powered
Headrests
Six-Way Power Seat
Radio
Trip Odometer
Twilight Sentinel
Cruise Control
Rear Window Defogger
Dimming Sentinel
Recliner
Tilt and Telescope Steering Wheel
Memory Seat
Remote Control Rearview Mirror (outside,
  electrically controlled)
Power Antenna

1960 *Thunderbird*

I f Ford had to scrap the two-seater in favor of a four-seater what better way than the "squarebird," as the second generation of T-Birds came to be called. It became the family sports car. With four separate bucket seats, center console, and that sculptured look. This was not only a style but also good design sense. When iron is given a slight fold or crease, its strength is geometrically increased. Try to push in on that sculptured iron, and then try and push in on the metal of a new car.

156

Specifications

Factory Price	$4,000	
Overall Length	205.3″	
Height	52.5″	
Width	77″	
Weight	3,813	
Engine	OHV V-8	OHV V-8 (optional)
	352 cid	430 cid
Bore & Stroke	4 × 3.5	4.3 × 3.7
Compression	9.6:1	10:1
Horsepower	300 @ 4,600 rpm	350 @ 4,400 rpm
Wheelbase	113″	
Suspension	coil front, leaf-spring rear	
Fuel Tank	20 gals	
Cooling System	20 qts	23 qts
Tires	8.00 × 14	8.00 × 14
Electrical	12 volts	
Frame	unitbody	
Carburetor	4 bbls	4 bbls
Axle Ratio	2.91:1 automatic	
	3.56:1 manual	
Transmission	manual/3-speed	
	manual/3-speed with overdrive	
	Ford-O-Matic	

The squarebird was made from 1958 to 1960. Among some of its features was a sun roof in the hardtop version.

157

Accessories

Power Steering
Power Brakes
Automatic Transmission
Heater/Defroster
Electric Clock
Six-Way Power Seat
Outside Mirror Driver's Side remote controlled
Power Windows
Air Conditioning
Power Trunk
Cruise Control
Automatic Headlight Dimmer
Radio
Power Antenna
Tilt Wheel
Rear Window Defogger
Power Door Locks
Spare Tire
Trip Odometer
Fuel and Temperature Gauges
Window Lock Switch
Sun Roof
Seat Belts

1962 *Thunderbird Roadster*

J ust when people were moaning that the T-Bird was starting to lose some of its "fun" appeal, Ford brought out the sports roadster. All it was in effect was the four-seat convertible with an optional fiberglass tonneau cover that went over the rear seats to give the car the look of a two-seat roadster. The unique disappearing convertible top could be raised and lowered with the tonneau in place.

If you needed the two extra seats, you had to put the top up and the tonneau in the trunk, and presto! Room

Specifications

Factory Price	$5,400
Overall Length	205"
Height	53.5" (Coupe 52.5")
Width	76"
Weight	4,471
Engine	OHV V-8
	390 cid
Bore & Stroke	4.05 × 3.78
Compression	9.5:1
Horsepower	300 @ 4,600 rpm
	385 @ 4,800 rpm
	405 @ 4,800 rpm
Suspension	independent coil front/leaf-spring solid axle rear
Fuel Tank	20 gals
Cooling System	19.5 qts
Tires	8.00 × 14
Electrical	12 volts
Frame	unitbody
Carburetor	single 4 bbls
	single 4 carb
	tri-power (three 2 bbls)
Transmission	automatic

for four. Not too many people knew this. T-Bird owners wanted the enjoyment of the car for themselves and a special companion.

The convertible top was stored in the trunk automatically. The rear deck lid would rise at the press of a button, the top would fold back out of sight, and the lid would then lower itself. Add Kelsey Hayes wire wheels and T-Bird red, and there's a Dream Machine!

One of the special features of the T-Bird was the

Accessories

Power Steering
Power Brakes self-adjusting
Automatic Transmission
Heater/Defroster
Electric Clock
Six-Way Power Seat each bucket
Outside Mirror Driver's Side remote controlled
Power Windows including vent
Air Conditioning
Power Trunk
Cruise Control
Automatic Headlight Dimmer
Radio
Power Antenna
Tilt Wheel swings away while entering or exiting
Rear Window Defogger
Power Door Locks
Spare Tire
Trip Odometer
Fuel and Temperature Gauges
Window Lock Switch
Seat Belts
Tonneau Cover changes convertible into 2-seat
    roadster

tilt-away steering wheel for ease of entry and exit. The tonneau would be made for two more years, the convertible for four. After 1966 there would be no more Thunderbird convertible.

In a June 1963 *National Geographic* advertisement for Thunderbird the headline is: "The Story of a Classic." The opposite page shows pictures of T-Birds from 1955 to 1963. The copy then goes on to describe an "American original," . . . "imitated—but unmatched." That's not just ad flak, it's the T-Bird.

The standard engine on the 1962 T-Bird was the 390 cid V-8. But there were two more engine options which very few people opted for. They were the 406 cid V-8 which put out 385 hp @ 4,800 rpm and 405 hp @ 4,800 rpm with the optional tri-power. Compression was raised to 11.4:1.

1962/64 *Cadillac Fleetwood 60*

A fter the 1959/60 Cadillac rocket-ship style, Cadillacs grew a little more conservative and classic. The 1964 is considered by some to be the best looking of postwar Caddys. Very pleasing from all angles, without being too chromey. Each year the fin grew a little smaller. The 1964 model would be the last to sport a tail fin.

From 1961 to 1964 the models were very similar. In 1961, the Fleetwood 60 took on a more formal roof line for

162

Specifications 1962 Cadillac

Factory Price	$10,000 (as equipped here)
Overall Length	222″
Height	56.3″
Width	79.9″
Weight	4,800
Engine	OHV V-8
	390 cid
Bore and Stroke	4 × 3.87
Compression	10.5:1
Horsepower	325 @ 4,800 rpm
Wheelbase	129.5″
Suspension	coil springs front and rear/front independent, rear solid axle
Fuel Tank	25 gals
Cooling System	19.75 qts
Tires	8.20 × 15
Electrical	12 volts
Frame	tubular X
Carburetor	4 bbls
Axle Ratio	2.94
Transmission	Hydramatic

Specifications 1964 Cadillac

Factory Price	$8,000 (as equipped here)
Overall Length	223″
Height	56.3″/coupe 55.1″ convertible 55.6″ limousine 59″
Width	79″
Weight	4,900
Engine	OHV V-8
	429 cid (7 liters)
Bore & Stroke	4.13 × 4
Compression	10.5:1
Maximum torque	480 ft lbs
Horsepower	340 @ 4,600 rpm
Wheelbase	129.5″
Suspension	independent front, coil springs/rear solid axle, coil spring
Fuel Tank	26 gals
Tires	8.20 × 15
Electrical	12 volts (55 amp gen)
Frame	tubular center X
Carburetor	4 bbls
Axle Ratio	2.94:1
Transmission	Turbo Hydramatic/torque converter type

Accessories 1962/1964 *Cadillac*

Power Steering
Power Brakes—self-adjusting
Automatic Transmission
Heater/Defroster
Electric Clock
Six-Way Power Seat
Cornering Lights
Outside Mirror Driver's Side remote controlled
Power Vent Windows
Air Conditioning
Power Trunk
Cruise Control
Automatic Headlight Dimmer
Radio/AM/FM (1964)
Power Antenna
Tilt Wheel
Twilight Sentinel automatic headlight regulator
Rear Window Defogger
Power Door Locks
Automatic Parking Brake Release
Spare Tire
Trip Odometer
Fuel and Temperature Gauges
Window Lock Switch
Seat Belts
Leather Interior
Bucket Seats sedan/coupe/convertible

a more elegant look. The 1962 was a cleaner model, more pleasing style. Its edges are not as rough as the 1961. By 1964 the Cadillac Fleetwood 60 offered anything and everything that is available today. From AM/FM radio to climate-control air conditioning and heating. You picked a temperature and set it, the thermostat in the car did the rest. Even the rear vent windows were power operated.

The 1964 Cadillac is the same length as the 1984 model, but it's five inches wider.

The 1964 Cadillac had a new engine, the 429 cid V-8. Although it was bigger than the 1963 it was lighter and could perform superbly. But Cadillac people took it for granted Cadillacs could perform.

At Daytona Beach in 1964 a brand new Cadillac with air conditioning was clocked at 118 mph. It was also checked for endurance. With the air conditioning on it circled the track for 75 minutes at 100 mph with no trace of trouble or any interior noise.

1962/63 *Lincoln Continental*

SIX THOUSAND, TWO HUNDRED AND SEVENTY DOLLARS

That was the headline for a 1963 Lincoln Continental ad as it appeared in November 1962. The car came with a two-year/24,000-mile guarantee. Not a protection plan, but a guarantee! Can you say that of any car today?

The Continental of 1961 to 1963 represented the height of postwar styling in a sedan and convertible (the convertible was a four door), a refreshing change after the hectic chrome-and-fin age.

Specifications 1962 Lincoln Continental

Factory Price	$7,600
Overall Length	212″
Height	53″ (sedan 55.5″)
Width	.78.6″
Weight	5,400
Engine	OHV V-8
	430 cid
Bore & Stroke	4.30 × 3.70
Compression	10.0:1
Horsepower	300 @ 4,100 rpm
Wheelbase	123″
Suspension	coil front/semi-elliptic leaf rear
Fuel Tank	21 gals
Cooling System	25 qts
Tires	9.50 × 14
Electrical	12 volts
Frame	unitbody
Carburetor	2 bbls
Transmission	automatic

Accessories

Power Steering
Power Brakes self-adjusting
Automatic Transmission
Heater/Defroster
Electric Clock
Six-Way Power Seat
Outside Mirror Driver's Side remote controlled
Power Windows including vent
Air Conditioning
Power Trunk
Cruise Control
Automatic Headlight Dimmer
Radio
Power Antenna
Tilt Wheel
Rear Window Defogger
Power Door Locks
Spare Tire
Fuel and Temperature Gauges
Window Lock Switch
Leather Interior

Specifications 1963 *Lincoln Continental*

Factory Price	$7,200
Overall Length	212″
Height	53.5″ (convertible 55″)
Width	78.6″
Weight	5,100
Engine	OHV V-8
	430 cid
Bore & Stroke	4.30 × 3.7
Compression	10.00:1
Horsepower	320 @ 4,600 rpm
Wheelbase	123″
Suspension	coil front/leaf-spring rear
Fuel Tank	21 gals
Cooling System	25 qts
Tires	9.50 × 14
Electrical	12 volts
Frame	unitbody
Carburetor	4 bbls
Transmission	automatic

Accessories 1963 *Lincoln Continental*

Power Steering
Power Brakes self-adjusting
Automatic Transmission
Heater/Defroster
Electric Clock
Six-Way Power Seat
Outside Mirror Driver's Side remote controlled
Power Windows including vent
Air Conditioning
Power Trunk
Cruise Control
Automatic Headlight Dimmer
Radio AM/FM
Power Antenna
Rear Window Defogger
Power Door Locks
Spare Tire
Trip Odometer
Fuel and Temperature Gauges
Window Lock Switch
Leather Interior standard on convertible
Seat Belts

From its center-opening rear doors to its squared-off front and wraparound taillights, the one phrase most often used to describe this new generation of Continentals was "distinguished looking." American taste was more secure, showiness was out.

The 1961 to 1963 Continental were almost identical. The 1961 and 1962 had the antenna mounted on the rear fender, driver's side. The 1963 had the antenna mounted on the front fender passenger side. The grilles were slightly different each year. The 1961 model was the last year of the 2¼″ wide whitewall. The following year would see the modern one inch stripe (the entire auto industry would change over also).

The biggest change in the Lincoln was its size . . . it had shrunk by more than one foot in length from the 1960 model. It was ten inches shorter than a Cadillac or Imperial and was considered a "luxury compact," for its time.

The Continental convertible was a marvel—completely automatic, with no hooks to unlatch. You just pressed a button and the top lowered itself into the trunk, leaving the car with a clean sweep of metal from any angle.

Here was a 5,200-pound car that could go from 0 to 60 in 9 seconds and yet surrounded you in rich leather and fine wood. The ride was incredible. "Refreshing to look at, excellence in design." The words still hold true today.

1963 *Ghia*

I n 1957 (like today), most new cars left the factory on giant transport trucks. This is an industry unto itself. One of the pioneers in the business was Gene Cassaroll of Detroit. During World War II Mr. Cassaroll had a contract with the government to transport huge bomber fuselages. For this work he devised a truck with two engines using mostly Dodge parts. From the use of two engines came the name Dual Motors.

Ghia is a custom body works in Turin, Italy. Gene

Specifications

Factory Price	$7,600	
Overall Length	212"	
Height	54"	
Width	77"	
Weight	3,500	
Engine	OHV V-8	OHV V-8 (optional)
	325 cid	352 cid
Bore & Stroke	3.69 × 3.80	3.94 × 3.63
Compression	10.00:1	10.00:1
Horsepower	260 @ 4,400 rpm	340 @ 5,200 rpm (dual quads)
Wheelbase	122"	
Suspension	torsion bar front/leaf-spring rear	
Fuel Tank	20 gals	
Cooling System	19 qts	
Tires	7.10 × 15	
Electrical	12 volt	
Frame	unitbody	
Carburetor	4 bbls dual quads (two 4 bbls)	
Transmission	Powerflite/automatic	

Accessories

Power Steering
Power Brakes
Automatic Transmission
Heater/Defroster
Electric Clock
Six-Way Power Seat individual buckets, fully reclining
Outside Mirror Driver's Side remote controlled
Power windows
Air Conditioning
Power Trunk
Cruise Control
Automatic Headlight Dimmer
Radio
Power Antenna
Rear Window Defogger
Power Door Locks
Spare Tire
Trip Odometer
Fuel and Temperature Gauges
Leather Interior

Cassaroll had a vision of a personal luxury-type car for the American market in the late 50s. Taking the Dodge chassis with the D-500 engine, he had them sent to Ghia to be custom-bodied to his specifications. The chassis were re-worked slightly and the result was the Dual Ghia, a car of exceptional elegance.

It came in two models—convertible and hardtop, and the early ones (1957 to 1960) had a slight fin. The Ghia was capable of speeds in excess of 120 mph and went from 0 to 60 in 8.6 seconds. It listed for $7,600.

The car was bought by many Hollywood celebrities, but this was not enough to sustain sales. The general public did not go for it ($7,600 was a lot of money for an unproven car). In today's market of personal luxury-type cars starting at $20,000, the Ghia would be right at home. In the late 50s and early 60s, it was a decade too soon.

1963 *Pontiac Tempest*

Four-wheel independent suspension, a transaxle with the transmission in the rear of the car, no hump in the floor, 50/50 weight distribution, the biggest four cylinder engine ever produced. Four cylinders for economy, 194 cubic inches for power when needed. That was the 1963 Tempest!**

 With its all-independent suspension the 1963 Tempest stays glued to the highway while delivering 26 mpg to 30 mpg, depending on conditions. With its 20-gallon fuel

Specifications

Factory Price	$2,600	
Overall Length	194.3"	
Height	54"	
Width	73"	
Weight	3,100	
Engine	OHV 4 cyl	OHV V-8
	194.5 cid	326
Bore & Stroke	4$\frac{1}{16}$ × 3$\frac{1}{4}$	3$\frac{25}{32}$ × 3$\frac{3}{4}$
Compression	1 bbl	2 bbls
	8.6:1	10.25:1
	120 @ 3,800 (automatic)	260 @ 4,800 rpm
Horsepower	115 @ 4,000 rpm (manual)	4 bbls
Wheelbase	112"	
Suspension	4-wheel independent transaxle	
Fuel Tank	20 gals	
Cooling System	12.6 qts (13 qts with a/c)	
Tires	6.50 × 15	
Electrical	12 volts	
Frame	unitbody	
Carburetor	1 bbl (2 bbls op/4 bbls op)	
Axle Ratio	standard/synchromesh	4 cyl 3.3:1
		8 cyl 3.09:1
		4 cyl 2.91:1
		8 cyl 2.69:1
Transmission	3-speed	a/c/all 3.56:1
	4-speed/op	
	Automatic/op	

Accessories

Power Steering
Power Windows
Automatic Transmission
Heater/Defroster
Electric Clock
Power Seat bucket driver's only
Remote Control Outside Mirror driver's side
Power Brakes
Air Conditioning
Spare Tire
Seat Belts
Bucket Seats
4-speed Floor Shift/Synchromesh
Tachometer
Radio two types, knob only, push button for pre-set
    stations
Trunk Light
Glove Compartment Light
Brakes Self-Adjusting

171

tank it put the worry out of always looking for a gasoline station.

The clean, crisp styling of the Tempest make it look like a fine "European" touring machine. Except for the $2,500 price and the Pontiac name, it could stand its own with any similar European product. Add the optional bucket seats and you truly have a grand "set of wheels!"

The 326 cubic inch V-8 is really just too much engine for this car. There is not enough road to accommodate it. Combine that 326 with four-speed synchromesh transmission and that little Tempest will take on any four-wheel brute that comes along!

Whether you were in it for just fifteen minutes or a long journey, the 1963 Tempest was FUN TO DRIVE. The brakes are automatically self-adjusting, everytime you back up and apply them they adjust themselves.

*The only other production car to use the rear-mounted transmission with 4-wheel independent suspension is a $40,000 Porsche. Either the Tempest was a tremendous bargain or the Porsche overpriced? Porsche came out with theirs 15 years after Pontiac.

1963 *Studebaker Avanti*

I n 1963 Studebaker was two years away from ceasing North American production. The Avanti was a last-ditch effort to revive interest and sales in the entire Studebaker line.

The Studebaker company had been started in 1852 by Henry and Clement Studebaker in South Bend, Indiana. Conestoga wagons was their original product line and they were once the world's major Conestoga producer. The Studebaker company remained in South Bend until 1965.

173

In its final years Studebaker was headed by Sherwood Egbert. In 1961 he asked Raymond Loewy to design a great automobile for Studebaker to revive sales. The result is the Avanti. It made its debut in 1963. In 1964 with fewer than 5,000 made, production was ended. The car looks as new today as in 1963.

In 1965, two South Bend businessmen, Nathan Altman and Leo Newman, bought the rights to the Avanti name and the die casts for the body from Studebaker. They set up the Avanti Motor Works and continued production in South Bend.

In 1982 they sold the Avanti II (as it appears on the

Specifications

Factory Price	$4,500	
Overall Length	194.4″	
Height	53.9″	
Width	70.4″	
Weight	3,365	
Engine	OHV V-8 (R-1)	OHV V-8 (supercharged/turbo) (R-2)
	289 cid	289 cid
Bore & Stroke	3⁹⁄₁₆ × 3⅝	3⁹⁄₁₆ × 3⅝
Compression	10.25:1	9.0:1
Horsepower	240 @ 4,500 rpm	289 @ 4,500 rpm
Wheelbase	109″	
Suspension	coil spring, independent front/leaf-spring, solid axle, rear	
Fuel Tank	18 gals	
Cooling System	19 qts	
Tires	6.70 × 15	
Electrical	12 volts	
Frame	iron chassis/fiberglass body	
Carburetor	4 bbls	
Transmission	4-speed manual	
	4-speed with overdrive/op	
	automatic/op	

Accessories

Power Steering
Power Brakes
Disc Brakes
Power Windows
AM/FM Radio
Air Conditioning
Heater/Defroster
Seat Belts
Tachometer
Electric Clock
Automatic Transmission
Underhood Light
Bucket Seats
Spare Tire
Fuel and Temperature Gauges
Tinted Glass
Windshield Washer

second generation of cars) to AMW Inc. Production is still based in South Bend.

The original Studebaker Avanti had a fiberglass body (and still does) and came with a 289 cid V-8 engine. This engine came in two versions, both with a 4-barrel carburetor. They were known as the R-1 and R-2, the difference being the R-2 was supercharged (or turbo as it is called today).

Round headlights set in a round housing typified the 1963 model—in 1964 the housing was square. The car's clean lines and understated appearance give it classic status.

1965 *Marlin*

The streamlined Marlin was American Motors' response to the burgeoning sporty car or pony car era, started with the introduction of the Mustang in late 1964. It was basically a two-door Rambler classic with the roof cut off and a fastback in its place. It was one of the first fastbacks to emerge in the mid-60s since their disappearance in 1950.

Equipped with either the 287 V-8 or the optional 327, this was quite a performance car with room for six and

176

Specifications

Factory Price	$3,100
Overall Length	195″
Height	55.3″
Width	71.3″
Weight	3,050
Engine	OHV V-8 OHV V-8
	327 cid 287 cid
Bore & Stroke	4 × 3.25 3.75 × 3.25
Compression	9.7:1 8.7:1
Horsepower	198 @ 4,700 rpm (2 bbls)
	270 @ 4,700 rpm (4 bbls)
	250 @ 4,700 rpm (2 bbls)
Wheelbase	112″
Suspension	coil springs, front and rear
Fuel Tank	20 gals
Cooling System	19 qts
Tires	7.50 × 14
Electrical	12 volts
Frame	unitbody
Carburetor	2 bbls/4 bbls op
Transmission	3-speed manual
	automatic op

Accessories

Power Steering
Front Disc Brakes
Automatic Transmission
Heater/Defroster
Electric Clock
Outside Mirror Driver's Side remote controlled
Power Windows
Air Conditioning
Cruise Control
Radio AM/FM
Power Antenna
Rear Window Defogger
Power Door Locks
Spare Tire
Trip Odometer
Fuel and Temperature Gauges

reclining front seats as standard equipment. It was supposed to be an image booster for AMC. In 1968 they would again come out with a new model, more in line with the "pony car" trend. Its name was the AMX.

The AMX was some car. When equipped with the 390 V-8 this car could hold its own with any muscle or foreign sports car. It too did not last. Neither car could shake AMC's basic Rambler/American image. Though the latter were well built, they weren't noted for "performance," and this carried over to the Marlin and AMX. It wasn't until after production stopped on these models that people realized how good they were. Today they are highly prized collectibles.

1965 *Studebaker Daytona*

T his was the final year for a South Bend Studebaker. In 1966 they would be assembled in Canada. After that there would be no more Studebaker name.

The 1965 Daytona is an interesting car from today's standpoint. Its size and engine would fit right in with contemporary downsized luxury cars. Those are real bucket seats, not simulated versions, with an armrest to separate them and create the bucket. The car lets you enter like a human being and visibility is superb. Today's rakish wind-

178

Specifications

Factory Price	$3,200
Overall Length	190″
Height	57″
Width	71″
Weight	3,000
Engine	OHV V-8
	283 cid
Bore & Stroke	$3\frac{7}{8} \times 3$
Compression	9.25:1
Horsepower	195 @ 4,800 rpm
Wheelbase	109″
Suspension	coil springs front/leaf springs rear
Fuel Tank	20 gals
Cooling System	18.5 qts
Tires	7.10 × 15
Electrical	12 volts
Carburetor	2 bbls
Transmission	3-speed manual synchromesh hydramatic/op

Accessories

Power Steering
Power Brakes
Automatic Transmission
Heater/Defroster
Electric Clock
Outside Mirror Driver's Side remote controlled
Power Windows
Air Conditioning
Cruise Control
Radio AM/FM
Power Antenna
Rear Window Defogger
Power Door Locks
Spare Tire
Trip Odometer
Fuel and Temperature Gauges
Seat Belts

shields may be wind-tunnel impressive, but they leave a lot to be desired in terms of looks.

The end of the line for Studebaker was the beginning of the line for today's new generation of luxury cars.

1966 *Mustang*

For those beings who are newly arrived on this planet, an announcement. In late 1964 Ford introduced a new car. Its name, MUSTANG. The results are the three cars seen here.

The Mustang spawned a generation of cars that were known as pony cars. The term applied to Camaros, Firebirds, AMX's, and Barracudas. But there is only one real pony, the Mustang.

Many people may not realize how old the Mustang is for they are still seen everywhere. The first generation was 1964–1966 but they seem to be just as new today.

180

Specifications

Factory Price	$2,400–$2,700		
Overall Length	181.6"		
Height	52.8"		
Width	74.1"		
Weight	coupe 2,488	fastback 2,520	convertible 2,650
Engine**	in line 6 cyl	OHV V-8 (op)	OHV V-8 (op)
	200 cid	289	289
Bore & Stroke	3.68 × 3.12	4 × 2.87	4 × 2.87
Compression	9.2:1	9.3:1	10.1:1
Carburetor	1 bbl	2 bbls	4 bbls
Horsepower	120 @ 4,400 rpm	200 @ 4,400 rpm	225 @ 4,800 rpm
Wheelbase	108"		
Suspension	coil front/leaf springs rear, solid axle		
Fuel Tank	16 gals		
Cooling System	18 qts		
Tires	6.50 × 13 (7.00 × 13/op, 7.00 × 14/op)		
Electrical	12 volts		
Transmission	3-speed manual 4-speed (on floor) optional automatic/optional		

**There was also an optional 289 cid with a bigger yet 4 barrel, putting out 271 @ 6,000 rpm, with compression at 10.5:1

Accessories

Power Steering
Power Brakes
Disc Brakes front only
Heater/Defroster
Outside Mirror Driver's Side remote controlled
Air Conditioning
Four-Speed Transmission
Automatic Transmission
Vinyl Roof
Tachometer
Seat Belts
Wire Wheel Covers
Tinted Glass
Power Convertible Top
GT Equipment Group dual exhausts, fog lamps, high performance V-8 disc brakes, GT racing stripes
Radio
Stereo Tape Player
Rear Deck Luggage Rack
Spare Tire

The first generation (1964–1966) sold 1,293,650 units. You could order it anyway you wanted . . . from an economical 6 cylinder to a high-performance 289 V-8. There was even a song named for the car—"Mustang Sally" sung by Wilson Pickett.

As the Thunderbird was growing beefier each year drivers were mourning the loss of the T-Bird spirit, the Mustang was born. If you look at the dimensions of the last two-seat Birds and compare them with the Mustang, you will see how close the two cars are. By taking a little off the long Thunderbird hood and making the Mustang's shorter, two seats could be fit into the rear of the Mustang—not spacious but adequate. It gave the car something extra that the original two-seater Bird did not have . . . not only sportiness, but room for four and small size as well. It was fun.

The Mustang was reasonably priced (started at $2,400) and easily serviced (witness how many are still around), and great looking!

In 1967 the Mustang got a slight style change (and a little bigger,) and sales went down a little too. In 1970 the third generation of Mustangs appeared—bigger and beefier without much more interior room or trunk space. In 1973, the final year for the original Mustang "look," sales totaled 134,000. In 1966 the Mustang had sold 607,300 units. The pony was gone from the Mustang.

1967 *Camaro* SS/69 *Camaro* Z-28

The introduction and success of the Mustang caught Chevrolet (and the auto industry) off guard. To counter Chevrolet brought out the Camaro in 1967. The Camaro came with a number of options and engines thus one could almost tailor-make a car. From the economical (and more than adequate) 6-cylinder to the potent 396 cid V-8, Camaro had a car for all drivers.

The Z-28 was a special high-performance car with a 302 cid V-8. The actual option package was called RPO Z-28. The Z-28 stuck and the RPO was left in the technical books. According to the guideline set down by the Sports

Specifications 1967 Camaro SS

Factory Price	$3,500
Overall Length	184.6"
Height	51"
Width	72.5"
Weight	3,200
Wheelbase	108"
Fuel Tank	18 gals
Cooling System	13 qts 6 cyl
	16 qts V-8
	23 qts V-8/396 cid
Crankcase	4 qts
	5 qts with oil filter
Tires	7.35 × 14 (optional 7.75 × 15)
Frame	unitbody
Electrical	12 volts
Transmission	3-speed manual
	4-speed floor shift, op
	powerglide 2-speed automatic op
	Turbo Hydramatic op

Engines Available

	6 cyl/in line 230 cid	6 cyl 250 cid	OHV V-8 327 cid	OHV V-8 327 cid	V-8 350	V-8 396	V-8 396
Carburetor	1 bbl	1 bbl	2 bbls	4 bbls	4 bbls	4 bbls	4 bbls
Horsepower	140 @ 4,400	155 @ 4,200	210 @ 4,600	275 @ 4,800	298 @ 4,800	325 @ 4,800	375 @ 5,600
Torque	220 @ 1,600	235 @ 1,600	320 @ 2,400	355 @ 3,200	380 @ 3,200	410 @ 3,200	415 @ 3,600
Compression	8.5:1	8.5:1	8.75:1	10.0:1	10.25:1	10.25:1	11.0:1
Bore	3.87	3.87	4	4	4	4.09	4.09
Stroke	3.25	3.53	3.25	32.5	3.48	3.75	3.76

Accessories 1967 *Camaro SS*

Power Steering
Power Brakes
Disc Brakes
Automatic Transmission
Four-Speed
Heater/Defroster
Rear Window Defogger
Outside Mirror Driver's Side
Power Windows
Air Conditioning
AM/FM Radio
Stereo Tape System
Tilt Steering Wheel
Vinyl Roof
Seat Belts
Shoulder Belts
Tinted Glass
Spare Tire
Folding Rear Seat
Strato Back Front Seat
Cruise Control
Full Instrumentation tachometer, fuel gauge,
    temperature gauge, ammeter, oil gauge
RS (Rally Sport) package: concealed headlights with
    vacuum-operated lids, special full-width grille
    with RS emblem* backup lights below rear
    bumper, parking/turn lights below front
    bumper, emblem on gas tank, RS script on
    front fender
SS (Super Sport) package: 350 or 396 engine, color
    keyed front accent band (black with light color,
    white with dark), red or white stripe tires,
    multi-leaf rear springs, black rear panel with
    396 engine, simulated air intakes on special
    hood, SS grille emblem*

*When the RS & SS packages were combined, SS
    emblems replaced the RS.

Car Club of America to be eligible to compete in its Trans-Am series of races, a car's engine could be no larger than 305 cid. The car also had to be a production car. The answer was the 302 V-8. Chevy took the 327 block with a four-inch bore and a 283 crankshaft with a three-inch stroke. Presto! A 302 cid Z-28.

The Z-28 could go from 0 to 60 mph in 7.4 seconds, cover the ¼ mile in 14.9 seconds with a speed of 101 mph, and had a top speed of 133. It cost $3,700.

The SS was a 350 cid that was a more practical version of a sporty street car. The Z-28, while it performed well, idled like a boat in heavy seas, and had a "slight" roar. The SS had more manners but was still able to perform . . . 0 to 60 was done in 7.8 seconds, it covered the quarter-mile in 15.8 seconds and topped out at 120 mph. In other words, it could still get you to work.

185

Why you may ask could the smaller engine perform better than the larger one? Now you are getting into headers, camshafts, and engineering, which an entire book devoted to the subject may or may not explain it all to you. The Z-28 was a high performance machine! That is why it sounded like it did while the SS was more sedate. That hood scoop on the Z-28 is not for looks but a functional cold-air induction system.

In 1968 the Camaro lost its front vent window, mainly to prevent break-ins and thefts (it was very easy to pop or break these small windows).

The original Camaros were produced from 1967 to 1969. In 1970 a new look was given the car which lasted

Specifications 1969 Camaro Z-28

Factory Price	$3,700
Overall Length	185″
Height	51″
Width	72.5″
Weight	3,100
Engine	OHV V-8* 302 cid
Compression	10.00:1
Horsepower	350
Wheelbase	108″
Suspension	coil springs front/leaf springs rear, solid axle
Fuel Tank	18 gals
Cooling System	13 qts 6 cyl/16 qts V-8 (396 V-8 23 qts)
Tires	F70 × 14 (E70 × 15 special performance on Z-28)
Electrical	12 volts
Frame	unitbody
Carburetor	4 barrel
Axle Ratio	3.73
Transmission	3-speed manual 4-speed/optional (standard on Z-28) automatic/optional

*The Z-28 was a special high performance 302 cid engine, with a heavy duty 4-speed, and power disc brakes. Dual exhausts were standard, with functional air scoop on hood.

until 1981. In 1982 a new look emerged with new electronic wizardry taking over many functions.

The Camaro unlike the Mustang has remained true to its concept its entire history. Whenever it changed body style it was always with the same thought. This is a 2-seater *and* a sporty car. After 1968, Mustang lost track of its original concept though, and never acquired the huge success of the first generation of Mustangs.

Today the early Camaros are highly prized and sought-after collector cars.

187

Accessories 1969 Camaro Z-28

Power Steering
Power Brakes
Power Disc Brakes
Four-Speed Heavy Duty Transmission (Z-28)
Automatic Transmission
Heater/Defroster
Air Conditioning
Power Door Locks
AM/FM Radio
Stereo Tape Deck
Rear Window Defogger electric wires
Tilt Steering Wheel
Vinyl Roof
Outside Mirror Driver's Side remote controlled
Power Windows
Seat Belts
Shoulder Belts
Tinted Glass
Folding Rear Seat
Strato Back Front Seat
Cruise Control
Full Instrumentation tachometer, fuel/temperature/
     oil/ammeter gauges
RS (Rally Sport) package
SS (Super Sport) package

1968 AMX

The AMX brought out by American Motors in 1968 was not just an effort by AMC to get into the "pony car" field but also to generate some interest in the entire AMC line. They hoped the AMX would bring people into dealer showrooms.

Craig Breedlove established many land-speed records with an AMX in 1968 at Goodyear's test track in Texas. Somehow the public did not believe that AMC could build a true performance car, and they did not "jam" dealer showrooms.

The AMX was a 2-seater. Whether its limited passenger space was a factor or whether it was just that it was

189

made by AMC, the car did not last long, remaining as a 2-seater only through 1970. Its larger rival, the Javelin, was continued in its place.

Today, the AMX is a highly appreciated pony car, eagerly sought after by people who know the car and its history, besides its great looks!

Specifications

Factory Price	$3,600		
Overall Length	177.2"		
Height	51.7"		
Width	71.6"		
Weight	3,163		
Engine	OHV V-8	OHV V-8	OHV V-8
	290 cid	343 (optional)	390 (optional)
Bore & Stroke	3.75 × 3.28		
Compression	10.0:1		
Torque	300 @ 3,200 rpm		
Horsepower	225 @ 4,700 rpm	280 @ 4,700 rpm	315 @ 4,700 rpm
Wheelbase	97"		
Suspension	independent coil, front/semi-elliptic springs, rear/Hyphoid solid axle		
Fuel Tank	17 gals		
Cooling System	14 qts		
Tires	E70 × 14		
Electrical	12 volts		
Frame	unitbody		
Carburetor	4 bbls		
Transmission	4-speed floor shift automatic op		

Accessories

Power Steering
Power Brakes
Disc Brakes
Automatic Transmission
Heater/Defroster
Electric Clock
Outside Mirror Driver's Side remote controlled
Power Windows
Dual Exhaust
Air Conditioning
AM/FM Radio
Stereo Tape Deck
Bucket Seats reclining
Spare Tire
Fuel and Temperature Gauges
Tachometer
Rally Paint Stripes

1970 *Pontiac* GTO

G TO . . . Muscle Car. To most performance-minded people they are one and the same. In 1964 Pontiac took a stock Tempest body, beefed up the suspension, put in a 389 cid engine, made tri-power an option, and the muscle-car era was born. The term muscle car refers to a medium-priced car in a medium-price range with a big engine. The suspension was usually a little stiffer so the car could handle reasonably well given its power to rate ratio.

There were big-engined cars before this, but the cars were large and expensive. The Mexican Road race

192

Specifications

Factory Price	$3,200	
Overall Length	202.5"	
Height	52.6"	
Width	76.7"	
Weight	3,700	
Engine	OHV V-8	OHV V-8 (optional)
	400 cid	455 cid
Compression	10.75:1	
Bore & Stroke	4.12 × 3.75	
Horsepower	350 @ 5,000 rpm	370 @ 5,400 rpm
Wheelbase	112"	
Suspension	coil springs, front and rear	
Fuel Tank	20 gals	
Cooling System	20 qts	
Tires	G70 × 14	
Electrical	12 volts	
Frame	unitbody	
Carburetor	4 bbls	
Transmission	3-speed manual	
	4-speed/floor shift (wide or close ratio)	
	Turbo Hydramatic	

Lincolns, the Chrysler 300 letter series, Desoto Adventurers, to name a few.

After 1966 tri-power was no longer available, but the engines grew larger until 1970 when there was an optional 455 cid in addition to the standard 400 cid. The car was growing each year too, not only in engine size but weight and length.

In 1969 Pontiac offered the Judge. This was a GTO with a rear spoiler (really did nothing unless the car was

Accessories

Power Steering
Power Brakes
Power Disc Brakes
Four-Speed Floor Shift/Synchromesh
Turbo Hydramatic
Bucket Seats
Outside Mirror Driver's Side remote controlled
Heater/Defroster
Air Conditioning
Power Windows
Electric Clock
AM/FM Radio
Tape Deck
Cruise Control
Tilt Wheel
Rear Window Defogger electric wires
Power Door Locks
Spare Tire
Power Trunk
Tinted Glass
Dual Exhaust
Full Instrumentation fuel/temperature/oil/ammeter
    gauges
Rear Deck Foil
Rally II Wheels
Side Stripes
Judge Stripes and Decals

doing 150 mph or more, which the car could not do to start with, and you would have to be crazy to attempt to do if you weren't a skilled race driver) and some decals and special striping. The cars also had Ram Air . . . these were functional hood scoops which took in cold air (which was really a lot of hot air advertising jargon).

Just as the Mustang was no longer what it started out to be the same was happening to the GTO. The 1970 GTO weighed 500 pounds more than the 1964 version.

Now for the answer to the question, what does GTO mean? The term goat is a generally accepted substitute for GTO. GTO . . . goat, get it?

But there really is a meaning for GTO. It is Italian for Gran Turismo Omologato. The term was used by several European manufacturers of high-priced performance cars . . . Ferrari being one. Pontiac took the initials and put them on their Tempest turned muscle car . . . GTO. A song (naturally) was named for the car by the group Rip Chords, "Little GTO."

1973 *Cadillac Eldorado*

For the 57th running of the Indy 500 a white Eldorado convertible was chosen as the pace car. This was a 500 cid engine coupled with front-wheel drive. Cadillac has used front-wheel drive on its Eldorados since 1967.

Unlike smaller compact cars with front-wheel drive that have their engines mounted crosswise under the hood, Cadillac's Eldorado had its engine mounted the conventional way—lengthwise.

195

Specifications

Factory Price	$8,800
Overall Length	222"
Height	54"
Width	79"
Weight	5,200
Engine	OHV V-8
	500 cid
Compression	8.5:1
Bore & Stroke	4.30 × 4.30
Horsepower	365 @ 4,400 rpm
Wheelbase	126.3"
Suspension	torsion bar front/coil springs rear
Fuel Tank	27 gals
Tires	L78 × 15
Electrical	12 volts/63 amp generator
Frame	perimeter type with boxed side rails
Carburetor	4 barrel
Axle Ratio	3.07:1
Transmission	Turbo Hydramatic

Accessories

Power Steering/Power Disc Brakes
Automatic Transmission/Cruise Control
Heater/Defroster
Electric Clock
Six-Way Power Seat
Cornering Lights
Outside Mirror Driver's Side and passenger side
    remote controlled
Power Windows
Air Conditioning
Power Trunk
Automatic Headlight Dimmer
Radio AM/FM stereo/Power Antenna
Tilt Wheel
Twilight Sentinel
Rear Window Defogger electric wires
Power Door Locks
Automatic Parking Brake Release
Spare Tire
Trip Odometer
Fuel and Temperature Gauges
Automatic Level Control
Seat Belts

The year 1973 also saw the first Middle East oil embargo. By 1974, 500-inch engines weren't in huge demand. The writing was on the wall. Within a decade the Cadillac engine would be halved, from the 8.2 liter (500 cid) to 4.1 liters (250 cid) in 1982.

The year 1973 was the last year the Cadillac 2-door hardtop would be, in effect, a hardtop. In 1974, the rear window in 2-door cars would no longer go up and down. Instead it would be fixed in place on the roof. The year 1976 would see the last of all hardtops, 2-door or 4-door.

Custom Cars

(CHOPPED, CHANNELLED, SECTIONED, LOWERED & LOUVERED)

A rather spectacular part of the 50s and early 60s car scene (and even of today's) was the "custom car." Oftentimes these specially designed super cars were thrown into the category of "hot rods," which they are not. The term "custom" does not refer to something that Detroit dreamed up, but rather an individual's own rendering of a particular auto. Although any car would do, most of the cars which inevitably wound up being customized were 1949–1951 Mercurys and Fords of the same time period.

If the owners of dream cars (I own several myself) have a few screws loose and are not running on all eight (their brain, not engine), custom owners definitely have a blown motor.

Here are terms that are essential to the customizer's vocabulary.

CHOPPED: involves the top part of the car—the glass, roof, and sitting area (or greenhouse, as it is sometimes called). Depending on the car and the individual designer varying amounts of inches are "chopped" off to lower the roof, accomplished by cutting the glass of the windshield.

LOWERED: lowering the suspension of the car. The amount is up to the person doing the lowering.

CHANNELLED: cutting out the floor of the car and raising it, thus enabling the car to be lowered even more. Extreme lowering almost guarantees channelling.

SECTIONING: major surgery that entails the slicing out of several inches of the car in its midsection, all the way around, for an overall lower look . . . the fenders, doors, firewall, dashboard are all sectioned and have various amounts taken out. This procedure entails the gutting of the car. The motor and interior are also removed. Sectioning is akin to double-by-pass with brain surgery at the same time.

LOUVERED: cutting louvers into hood. Although this procedure enables the heat from the engine to escape, it also allows rain water in if the louvers are not rigged with some mechanism to close them during a storm.

Put this all together and you have the leadsled. The term lead sled refers to the lead covering all the welds where the sheet metal was cut to be channelled, chopped, or sectioned. The lead makes a smooth surface when done properly, enabling the car to be painted (preferably some exotic color).

197

Leadsleds are handcrafted cars. They are the ultimate form of creativity and individuality in cars. The people who design and craft them are truly artisans and craftspeople in the highest form. While Detroit has committees spending years (and huge amounts of money) to design and build a sometimes functional automobile, the customizers work with a given form and rework it in a small garage without a blueprint, just their imagination and design talent.

Many of the cars brought out by Detroit in the mid- and later 50s were modified versions of custom street cars.

Headlights with extended one-piece fenders over them (Frenched), curved glass, smooth or recessed door handles. Many customs have no door handles, but buttons on the bottom of the door. Hidden gas caps (usually in a taillight—which Cadillac is famous for). Skirts were used extensively to give cars a low and smooth look. These and other design trends started with individual custom cars or lead sleds!

The 1955–1960 period of American cars and their designs cannot be written about or photographed without some understanding of lead sleds and their effect on Detroit styling boards.

The 1950 Mercury (lime green) and 1957 Olds illustrated in this book are owned by Joel Sheipe of New York. Joel, from all outward appearances, seems to be a normal human being. But looks can be deceiving. He owns these cars! What kind of normal human behavior is that?

I would like to thank Joel for letting me photograph his two "dream machines," and for enlightening me about low riders, custom cars, and lead sleds. The license plate on his Mercury says it all. I would also like to thank Joel for letting me drive his leadsled. It boosted my ego about a mile high for that short ride.

1950 *Custom Mercury (Leadsled)*

T he basic car specifications are given for the standard 1950 Mercury in this book. What follows is what has been done to this particular vehicle.

V-D WINDSHIELD: very few cars of this time period had a one-piece windshield. To give the effect of a one-piece window, the post separating the two halves was taken out and the glass beveled and custom fitted together in a V shape, called veed.

Specifications

Overall Length	206.3″
Height	56″
Width	73″
Weight	3,700
Engine	OHV V-8
	350 cid (Chevy engine)
Bore & Stroke	4.00 × 3.48
compression	9.00:1
Horsepower	250 @ 4,500 rpm
Wheelbase	118
Suspension	coil front/semi-elliptic springs rear
Fuel Tank	19 gals
Tires	H-78 × 15
Electrical	12 volt
Carburetor	two barrel
Transmission	4-speed

Accessories

Power Steering
Power Brakes
Automatic Transmission
Heater/Defroster
Electric Clock
Six-Way Power Seat
Air Conditioning
Power Trunk
Cruise Control
Radio AM/FM stereo
Power Antenna
Tilt Wheel
Rear Window Defogger
Power Door Locks
Spare Tire—Full Size
Trip Odometer
Fuel and Temperature Gauges
Button to Open Door on underside of body where door meets body

1950 FORD TAILLIGHTS (Blue dots): Why use Ford taillights? Why not. This was what the customizer felt was appropriate.

FRENCHED HEADLIGHTS WITH CATSEYES: the chrome half moons over the headlights are known as "catseyes." Frenched refers to the rounded seamless effect of the fender over the light.

ROUNDED HOOD CORNERS: just what it says.

1955 DESOTO GRILLE: nice and toothy.

CHOPPED: 4½ inches: the roof (and glass area) had 4½ inches taken out—but since this is nifty fifty car you do not lose any interior headroom due to the curvature of the roof.

FRENCHED ANTENNA
VELOUR & NAUGAHYDE INTERIOR
350 C.I.D. Chevy engine
4-speed Chevy Transmission
No door handles on exterior

1957 *Custom Oldsmobile* (Precious & Few)

This lowered and louvered Olds is basically a stock Olds. That is, the motor and transmission are the original rocket Olds. Even the color, outlandish as it may seem, is a stock 1958 Olds color. What separates this Olds from the standard stock Olds is:

CHOPPED 3½ inches: the roof and glass (curved glass too) were cut 3½ inches. How do you cut curved glass . . . VERY CAREFULLY!

202

Specifications

Overall Length	208.2"	98 216.7"
Height	58.2"/stock (Custom 52.2")	
Width	76.38"	
Weight	4,119	4,458
Engine	OHV V-8	OHV-8
	371 cid	371 cid
Bore & Stroke	4 × 3.69	4 × 3.69
Compression	9.5:1 standard/J-2 optional	
	10:00:1	
Horsepower	277 (300 optional J-2)	
Wheelbase	122"	126"
Suspension	coil front, semi-elliptic rear	
Fuel Tank	20 gals	
Cooling System	21.5 qts	
Tires	8.00 × 14	
Electrical	12 volts	
Carburetor	four barrel/J-2 option this was a 3 two-barrel set-up which was 300 hp and 10.00:1 compression	
Axle Ratio	3.23:1 automatic	
Transmission	3-speed manual standard Hydramatic option on 88	

Accessories

Power Steering
Power Brakes
Automatic Transmission
Heater/Defroster
Electric Clock
Six-Way Power Seat
Outside Mirror Drivers Side remote controlled
Power Windows
Air Conditioning
Power Trunk
Automatic Headlight Dimmer
Radio . . . Sportable
Power Antenna
Rear Window Defogger
Power Door Locks
Spare Tire
Trip Odometer
Fuel and Temperature Gauges

LAKE PIPES: these are the chrome pipes on the bottom of the car. They look like exhaust pipes, but are not.

DUAL FRENCHED ANTENNAS

1956 OLDS GRILLE

ROLLED & PLEATED INTERIOR

LOWERED: the car has been lowered to within 2 inches of the pavement. It has air shocks to raise it up when necessary. (Some customs have hydraulic lifters installed to raise the car when necessary. This system is more effective—and more costly.)

LOUVERED HOOD: the slits or louvers in the hood.

204

Appendixes

Where to Find a Car

There is no one special place to find a dream machine, although I personally believe that every car ever made is in New Jersey and Pennsylvania. New Jersey has an incredible amount of old tin that people still use. Most of it is in good shape, too. The state motor vehicle commission seems to recognize the value (not only monetary but emotional) that people place on old cars and makes it easy for them to get antique plates and to register as such.

There are numerous shows and flea markets that are listed in the publications that serve the car enthusiast. Go to these shows and get a feeling for what is being asked for the cars and what they are selling for. Also, note the difference in quality from car to car.

Another tip: Buy the local paper and numerous other local publications that serve people selling merchandise. Each area has its own. In the New York/New Jersey area some noted publications are "Want Ads," "Buy Lines," and "Selling Post." Find out about the publications in your area.

A special word about the spectacular Hershey and Carlisle auto shows in the fall. The shows are usually the last weekend of September and the first weekend in October. Carlisle started as an outgrowth of Hershey. The Antique Auto Club of America (AACA) did not recognize cars of the post-World War II period, in the early 1970s. Two unrelated men with the same last name, the Miller boys, started Carlisle for the "orphan" people with 50s cars. Today Carlisle has about 7,000 vendors and sells almost anything for your post-World War II dream machine. In addition, there is a field where over 2,000 cars are for sale, swap, or whatever. It is pure capitalism and individualism, give or take 70,000 people.

Hershey is the grandaddy of car meets or shows. It now has a show area of about 1,500 cars that are twenty-five years or older. Older can mean down to a 1903 Olds and usually there are more than one.

In addition, there are 7,500 vendors selling anything and everything for old cars and trucks. Try to imagine a square mile filled with over 200,000 people, 7,500 stalls of car parts surrounded by hillsides covered with cars for sale. Hershey (Carlisle, too) is a place where the "farmer" in overalls and a pickup beside his stall may just own five acres in Greenwich which happens to be the home of thirty or so cars plus a house.

It is where the person with a Duesenberg three rows over passes your 1951 Rambler and says, "nice car," and means it! When asked if he had one he would say yes, and not brag about his Deuce three rows back.

These two weekends are filled with white teeth and smiles and no toothpaste commercials are being made.

How to Find a Car

In addition to some of the ways mentioned in Where to Find a Car, one of the best methods is to buy an old car. This does not mean to buy a first-class car . . . just buy any old car to start with. As long as it runs and does not smoke. It is amazing how much easier it is to stop someone who is driving a car you may want when you are driving an old car yourself—even if it is in bad shape.

Owning an older car will also help you acquire a taste for what you can and cannot expect from one. Usually you will have a more dependable car than you thought possible with less headaches.

There is always an old couple ready to sell off their Pontiac sedan or Plymouth at a reasonable price. With a little work the shine can be brought back to the paint, the chrome polished, and a set of whitewalls will add a little beauty to what was a drab machine when you bought it. This little machine will take you to car shows, to auctions, into people's hearts . . . until the day when you see your dream machine.

How to Restore a Car

Restoring a car can mean anything from replacing a hubcap or getting the proper white-wall width for the tires, to completely dismantling the auto down to the chassis and rebuilding everything—the motor, the pumps, the wiring—and finally repainting in a factory color for that year of car. There are many different opinions on repainting but as a guide (and according to the AACA) it means to bring the car back to its original color. Don't overdo it though; no car ever came with twenty coats of paint.

There is also the matter of restoring for "show" or "go." Cars were meant to be driven (even if only once a month) so as far as this author is concerned it is much better to restore for "go" than "show."

This may mean that if you like a particular shade of blue, or red, and it was not available for your car at the time it was manufactured—go ahead and use it. The key word to this hobby is *fun!* When it ceases to be fun, get out. I know several people who own thirty or more cars. They get as much fun out of driving their clunkers as well as their "show" cars. One collector who owns over thirty cars, including a few Rolls's, drives a 1950 Hudson every day—because it's *fun*.

The difference between a "restoration" shop and an ordinary mechanic is that a restoration shop is prepared to keep a car for an extended period of time (up to a year) to complete the work. They will undertake all mechanical and body work (you also pay for this). Instead of looking for a body shop, a shop that specializes in interiors (most restoration shops give out this work to very competent people), and a mechanical shop, a restoration shop undertakes all this work.

You can also check around in your local community for a competent mechanic, a good body shop, and an interior shop. It is not that hard to find these specialty shops, and you can then pay as you go—and drive your car between visits.

The various periodicals devoted to the hobby have ads from restoration shops.

How to Find Parts, Supplies, and Repair Shops

Almost any part I have found is available locally, if one wants to invest a little time and effort and brainpower.

By time and effort this means that after one phone call you do not give up. It may taken ten phone calls, but the part you want will be available somewhere. Effort means the physical energy spent to look up the dealers, parts houses, junkyards, etc. in your area that may have some knowledge about your vehicle.

Brainpower means that one uses the thing between their shoulders to know what they are looking for and try to have all part numbers of the part they are trying to replace. Some models from the same year would have different master cylinders, for example. Know which part you need for your car. You should know if you have a 6 or 8 or V-8 cylinder engine and the size of your engine. Many parts vary depending on the size of the engine.

After all this (or before this if you mind "wasting" your time) the following is just a small group of people who are reliable, courteous, and knowledgeable. As for price, that is for you to find out. But remember these people make a living at their particular business and they depend on repeat business to maintain their growth.

I have dealt with these businesses and have found them to be reliable. I live in the New York City area and cannot say anything about any area or shop I have not dealt with. If you obtain the part you need, the corner mechanic can do the repair work. Old cars are usually simpler to work on than newer ones!

KANTER AUTO PRODUCTS
Monroes Street
Boonton, NJ 07005
800/526-1096

Fred and Dan started out supplying parts for Packards. They now have the world's largest inventory of Packard parts. In addition they also have many mechanical parts for most American cars . . . old cars that is. They can also supply you with leather hides and paint for cosmetic restoration.

BILL HIRSCH (no relation!)
396 Littleton Avenue
Newark, NJ 07103
201/642-2404
Can supply you with Packard parts. In addition has large supply of paints, convertible top material, upholstery material, wheel trim rings, etc.

JOHN KEPICH/exhaust systems
Box 115, 544 East Main Street
East Orwell, OH 44034
216/437-8622
216/352-7990
Has in stock and can make any exhaust system for almost any car.

POWER TRANSMISSION
3099 Cropsey Avenue
Brooklyn, NY 11224
Can rebuild transmissions and also supply parts for same.

VINTAGE PARTS HOUSE
93 Whippany Road
Morristown, NJ 07960
201/539-5307
Has mechanical parts for mostly GM cars 1936 and up.

BATTERY SPECIALISTS OF NEW YORK
369-375 Park Avenue   82 Allen Boulevard
Brooklyn, NY 11205   East Farmingdale, NY 11735
718/UL2-0555-0574   516/752-0011
Has old style black rubber batteries in 6 and 12 volt.

A-ONE TRANSMISSION PARTS
653 11th Avenue
New York, NY 10036
212/581-7490
Transmission and only transmission parts . . . very good.

SURPLUS & OBSOLETE
1125 Hamilton
Philadelphia, PA 19123
Has mechanical parts for AMC cars 1956 and up.

DAVID FICKEN/windshield wipers, parts, and motors (TRICO)
Box 11
Babylon, NY 11702
516/587-3332
Has large supply of TRICO wiper motors and can rebuild almost any old wiper motor you have.

AUTO PARTS EXCHANGE
P.O. Box 736
Reading, PA 19603
215/372-2813 after 6 PM
215/921-9339 Wed. to Sat. 10 AM to 2 PM
Specializes in Lincoln parts from 1958–1979.

BEVERLY HILLS CAR COVERS
200 South Robertson Boulevard
Beverly Hills, CA 90211
800/421-0911
In California call 213/657-4800
Makes car covers for any car. Covers are all cotton with Scotchgard. (I personally prefer all cotton.)

RELIABLE CAR COVERS
1751-H Spruce St
Riverdale, CA 92507
800/854-4770
In California call 714/781-0261
Makes poly/cotton car covers.

HIBERNIA AUTO RESTORATION
Maple Terrace
Hibernia, NJ 07842
201/627-1882
Can tune up a car to a complete frame up restoration from a 1951 Rambler to a 1936 Packard.

ROBERT GASSAWAY/complete restorations
Perth Amboy, NJ 08861
From a Duesenberg to a Dodge.

MAX PENN & SON
219 Johnson Avenue
Brooklyn, NY 11206
718/497-1333
    Auto interiors, convertible tops. In business 60 years. What they forgot most people do not even know.

LEOGRANDE
171 Hope Street
Brooklyn, NY 11211
718/384-7088
    Mechanical repairs and painting. American cars only, thinks FORD stands for: Fix Or Repair Daily.

HUBCAP STORE
Easton, PA 215/252-1421
New Brunswick, NJ 201/846-8352
    Wheelcovers and hubcaps for almost any car.

RNA AUTOMOTIVE
1010 Oakley Park Road
Walled Lake, Michigan 48088
800/922-1128
    Reproduction rubber parts.

SURPLUS & OBSOLETE AUTOMOTIVE
Box 10
Bridgeport, PA 19404
    Water pumps, wiper motors, carburetors for most cars.

RESTORATION SPECIALTIES & SUPPLY INC.
P.O. Box 328 R.D. 2
Windber, PA 15963
    Window channels, trim moldings, door and trunk weatherstripping.

JUST SUSPENSION
P.O. Box 167
Towaco, NJ 07082
201/335-0547
    American Cars 1937–1979
    Ball joints, tie rod ends, king pins, bushings, etc.

How to Insure an Old Car

"Does it cost a fortune to insure all those old cars? Do you have all those cars insured? Can you get all those cars insured?" Those are the three most asked questions by people who are not in the hobby of old cars. The answers are no, yes, and yes!

Insurance brokers and sales agents usually know less about antique/special-interest car insurance than the person who is inquiring about the insurance. Someone who is selling new car insurance usually knows very little or nothing about antique insurance. I was lucky with my first car. I asked my broker and he inquired about such a policy and insured the car, no hassle!

The following are agents who are reputable. Several years ago there was a company that advertised something like, "No license? We'll insure you. Eighteen speeding tickets? No problem, still get our famous low rates." The catch was you got low rates and *no* insurance. They were taking people's money, but were not writing any legitimate policies. That is not what I mean by reputable. Either contact the company on your own or have your broker do so. The company I refer to is no longer in existence and did *not* insure antique/special-interest vehicles.

The companies listed here are knowledgeable and courteous. They will answer any question you have.

CONDON & SKELLY
Beverly-Rancocas Road
P.O. Box Drawer A
Willingboro, NJ 08046
800/257-9496
609/871-1212 (in New Jersey)

AMERICAN COLLECTORS
P.O. Box 720
214 Main Street
Moorestown, NJ 08057
800/257-5758

THE GRUNDY AGENCY
501 Office Center Drive
Fort Washington, PA 19034
215/628-3100

J. C. TAYLOR
220 South 69th Street
Upper Darby, PA 19082
800/345-8290
800/552-3535 (in Pennsylvania)

How to Determine the Value of an Old Car

There are a few publications that are printed every year to use as a guide to buying a car. One that is published quarterly is *Old Car Price Guide*. It is just that, a guide. It gives an average pricing taken from auctions and dealers.

Dealers like to say that certain cars increase in value 20 percent a year. They are in

211

business and they have to make money. This is not a criticism of them, but if you buy a car from one at $10,000, you can bet the dealer will not buy it back from you at the end of the year for $12,000!

This author knows of a person who bought a 1960 T-Bird convertible for $7,500 and had to sell it a year later for $3,500. Then there is the person who paid $5,000 for a 1953 Pontiac sedan (in close to showroom condition) who probably could not get more than $3,000 for it—and that person does not care. He and his wife love the car. They do not want to sell it so they don't care what it is worth. There is also the person who bought a 1961 Corvette for $3,500 and sold it a year later for $6,000. He did not sell it to make a profit but to buy another car. He was offered $6,000 and sold it.

If you buy a car you like, at a price you think is fair—and drive the car and have fun and maintain it—you will never lose money, and will probably make some when you do sell it.

From what this author has seen, you could buy a car today, and in five years probably sell it for 50 percent more than you paid for it. You can drive it, enjoy it, have fun, and make a profit. You cannot do that with any new car made today by anyone.

This does not happen everyday . . . but I know a person who purchased a used Duesenberg in 1950 for $300. In 1959 he sold it for $7,000 and was the happiest person in the world. The same car sold recently for $120,000. In 1950 no one wanted the Deuce. Don't be afraid of buying the car you like!

Car Publications

The following publications are worth looking at to broaden one's knowledge of the old car hobby, not only to find parts, but to have a ballpark value of cars and to find out when and where there are shows and meets.

The two biggest meets are in Hershey and Carlisle, Pennsylvania in the fall every year. The dates are given in *Hemmings Motor News* and *Old Cars Weekly*.

HEMMINGS MOTOR NEWS (The Bible!)
Box 100
Bennington, VT 05201

CARS & PARTS
911 Vandemark Road
Sidney, OH 45365

OLD CARS WEEKLY
700 East State Street
Iola, WI 54990

OLD CARS PRICE GUIDE
Same as Old Cars Weekly . . . quarterly magazine and is a guide, not an official price list of cars. Most insurance companies use the guide as a basis for insuring a car.

BOOKS

THE AMERICAN AUTOMOBILE
by John B. Rae
University of Chicago Press

THE SURVIVOR SERIES
by Henry Rasmussen
Silverado Publications/Motor Books International

Glossary

a/c Air conditioning.

bbls Refers to the carburetor's number of barrels.

Bore and Stroke Diameter of the cylinder and the length of the piston's stroke from top to bottom.

C.I.D. Cubic inch displacement. This represents the volume size of the engine.

Coil Springs Just that, a coil spring.

Compression Ratio The ratio between the volume of the cylinder when the piston is all the way up and when it is all the way down. As combustion gets smaller, the ratios tend to get higher. The higher the compression, the more efficiently the fuel is burned. But this also requires a higher grade of gasoline which translates into more expensive gasoline. Sometimes referred to as anti-knock or just higher octane gasoline.

Coupe Before the hardtop, this referred to a sporty two-door car.

Dual Exhausts (twin exhaust) Two mufflers and two sets of exhaust pipes. Twice the headaches of single exhaust (and more money).

Dual Quads Two four-barrel carburetors.

Fastback Style of two-door popular in the 1930s and 1940s. With the hardtop's coming the fastback or sedanette was dropped. Fastback came back into vogue in the mid 70s.

Hardtop A pillarless car. No posts between front door and rear door (or front and rear window). 1949 was the first year of the two-door hardtop and 1955 was the first year of the four-door hardtop. The year 1976 was the last year for all hardtops.

Hardtop Convertible The pillarless car that came into being in the early 50s, made to resemble a convertible. The only true hardtop convertible was the Ford Skyliner of 1957–1959.

Horsepower The maximum horsepower an engine will develop under certain favorable laboratory conditions, without such accessories as exhausts, air conditioning, power equipment (steering, brakes), etc. Optional power equipment can reduce a car's maximum horsepower from 25 to 50 percent!

Hydramatic Another term for automatic transmission.

Land Yacht Refers to a big (Buick, Caddy, Lincoln) chrome machine of the 50s.

Leaf Springs Straight springs with a slight curve and placed on top of each other, usually more rigid than a coil spring.

Manual Shift Shift with stick and clutch. Could be floor- or column-mounted on steering wheel.

Maximum Torque The amount of turning force exerted at the flywheel by the engine which makes the power-wheels turn (rear-wheel or front-wheel drive).

Muscle Car Relatively light weight car with a big engine and heavier suspension so the car could handle reasonably well given its power-to-weight ratio.

n/a Not available.

Pony Car You may hear this expression and wonder what it means. It implies a small (not compact) sporty car that holds two people up front comfortably and two in the rear not so comfortably. The name came into being when Ford brought out its original Mustang in late 1964 (1964½) . . . Mustang thus the word *pony*. This was a fun car that could be ordered to one's personal taste and driver preference. There was a basic 200 cid six-cyl. engine up to the 289 with a four-barrel. The first six cylinders were 170 cid which in 1965 grew to 200 cid. It was either a fun car that was economical to drive or a gutsy sporty car that could give quite a few European "touring" cars a run for their money . . . and at thousands less. At 181" it was the same length as the last two-seater T-Bird in 1957. (The 55 and 56 were 175".) It was a visually exciting car to look at and to drive, and fairly easy to maintain mechanically. Ford Motor Company has contributed a few words to the English language. Say Edsel and to most people it implies a major blunder, a *big mistake*. Say T-Bird and imaginations light up with a sporty two-seater car and a luxurious four-seater convertible of the late 50s and early 60s. (Even Ford knows this. They are still running their modern T-Bird on the powerful image of the 50s.) *Pony* Car is another expression Ford has contributed to our language, and what a car it was and still is. Two out of three is not bad!

Pop-up Headlights The 1936 Cord had them.

Rear-axle Ratio The number of turns of the driveshaft necessary to make both rear wheels (rear-wheel drive) complete one full revolution. The lower the ratio, the fewer times the engine revolves per mile traveled and the better the fuel economy. The larger the ratio, the better the get-away of the car from a stop and the better the car can go up a steep grade without downshifting . . . but again less fuel economy.

Shipping Weight Weight of the car without optional equipment, gasoline, or water. Curb weight is more.

Tin or Old Tin Commonly refers to old cars.

Tri-Power Three dual-barrel carburetors.

Wheelbase The distance from the center of a front wheel to the center of a rear wheel. Usually the longer the wheelbase the better the ride.

Yank Tank What Europeans fondly call large American cars.

National Car Club Listing

General Interest

American British Cab Society
4470 Cerritos Avenue
Long Beach, CA 90807

Antique Automobile Club of
America (50,000 members)
501 W. Governor Rd.
Hershey, PA 17033

The Classic Car Club of America
P.O. Box 443
Madison, NJ 07940

Classic Contemporary Car Club
P.O. Box 576
Birmingham, MI 48013

Contemporary Hist. Vehicle
Assoc.
P.O. Box 40
Antioch, TN 37013

Historical Automobile Society of
Canada
820 York Road, RR2
Guelph, Ontario, N1H 6H8
Canada

Horseless Carriage Club of Amer.
6 Harold's Circle
Richardson, TX 75081

International Antique Auto Club
905 McCandless Street
Sault Ste Marie, MI 49783

Milestone Car Society
P.O. Box 50850
Indianapolis, IN 46250

National Street Rod Assoc.
3041 Getwell No. 301
Memphis, TN 38118

Veteran Motor Car Club
105 Elm St.
Andover, MO 01810

Specialized Clubs

AMERICAN MOTORS MODELS

AMC Rambler Club
2645 Ashton Rd.
Cleveland, OH 44118

American Motors Drag Racers
Ass'n
1524 Silver Strand Circle
Palatine, IL 60067

American Motors Owners Assoc.
1615 Purvis Ave.
Janesville, WI 53545

Marlin Owners Club
RD 5 Box 187
Coatesville, PA 19320

Classic AMX Club Int'l
501 Indian Terrace
Rockford, IL 61103

Classic AMX Club
1135 Bloomfield Rd.
San Pedro, CA 90732

Amphicar
14330 Iseli Road
Santa Fe Springs, CA 90670

Auburn-Cord-Deusenberg Club
RD 6 Box 483
Rome, NY 13440

AUSTIN-HEALEY MODELS

Austin-Healey Club
603 E. Euclid Avenue
Arlington Heights, IL 60004

Austin-Healey Sports & Touring
P.O. Box 3539
York, PA 17402

NA Auto Union Register
1023 Los Trancos Road
Portola Valley, CA 94025

Avanti Owners Ass'n Int'l
P.O. Box 296
Westminster, CO 80090

Berkeley Exchange
46 Elm Street
North Andover, MA 01845

BUICK MODELS

Buick Club of America
P.O. Box 898
Garden Grove, CA 92642

Buick Compact Club of America
Rt. 1 Box 39B
Marion, TX 78124

McGlauglin-Buick Club
333 Centennial Road
West Hill, Ontario, M1C 2A4
Canada

1932 Buick Registry
3000 Warren Rd.
Indiana, PA 15701

1966-67 Riviera Directory
Box 825
Dearborn, MI 48121

Buick GS Club of America
1213 Gornto Road
Valdosta, GA 31602

CADILLAC MODELS

Cadillac-LaSalle Club
3340 Poplar Dr.
Warren, MI 48091

Cadillac Club
507 E. Walnut
Ripley, MS 38663

Cadillac Club International
Box One
Palm Springs, CA 92263

Cadillac Convertible Owners of
Amer.
P.O. Box 920
Thiells, NY 10984

Brougham Owners Assoc.
1957-60 Eldorado Broughams
829 W. Wesley St.
Atlanta, GA 30327

Cartercar Club
10208 Aviary Drive
San Diego, CA 92131

Checker Car Club of America
469 Tremaine Ave.
Kenmore, NY 14217

Cheetah Registry
956 Calle Primavera
San Dimas, CA 91773

CHEVROLET (CORVETTE,
CORVAIR & CAMARO)

Early Four Cylinder Chev Club
P.O. Box 62
San Leandro, CA 94557

National Chevelle Owners Assoc.
P.O. Box 5014
Greensboro, NC 27435

National Nomad Club
4691 Mariposa Dr.
Englewood, CO 80110

Classic Chevy Club Int'l
(1955-1957 cars)
P.O. Box 17188
Orlando, FL 32860

Tri-Chevy Assoc.
431 Caldwell
Chicago Hts. IL 60411

1955-57 Chevy Owners Assoc.
157 Coram-Mt. Sanai Rd.
Coram, NY 11727

Vintage Chevrolet Club of Amer.
P.O. Box 5387
Orange, CA 92667

National Impala Assoc.
P.O. Box 968
Spearfish, SD 57783

Late Great Chevy Club
(1958-1964 cars)
P.O. Box 17824
Orlando, FL 32860

National 409 Chevy Club
2510 E. 14th St.
Long Beach, CA 90804

Corvair Society of Amer.
2506 Gross Point Road
Evanston, IL 60201

National Corvette Owners Assoc.
P.O. Box 777A
404 South Maple Ave.
Falls Church, VA 22046

National Corvette Restorers
Society
6291 Day Road
Cincinnati, OH 45247

National Council of Corvette
Clubs
P.O. Box 325
Troy, OH 45373

Corvette Club of America
P.O. Box 30223
Washington, D.C. 20814

Int'l Registry of Early Corvettes
P.O. Box 666
Corvallis, OR 97339

National Nostalgic Nova
(1962-1979 Chevy Nova)
P.O. Box 943
York, PA 17405

Camaro Owners of Amer.
701 N. Keyser Ave.
Box 961
Scranton, PA 18501

U.S. Camaro Club
P.O. Box 24489
Huber Heights, OH 45424

Cosworth Vega Owners Assoc.
P.O. Box 910
22032 Trailway Lane
El Toro, CA 92630

Super Chevy Ltd.
P.O. Box 6657
Lakeland, FL 33807-6657

The Chevy Association
Box 172
Elwood, IL 60421

The 1965-66 Full Size Chevy
126 Charles Road
Southampton, PA 18966

International Camaro Club, Inc.
P.O. Box 81342
Chamblee, GA 30366

CHRYSLER (DESOTO, DODGE,
PLYMOUTH)

Airflow Club of Amer.
2029 Minoru Drive
Altadena, CA 91001

Barracuda Owners Club
167 Clarence
Torrington, CT 06790

Chrysler Products Owners
3511 Madison Place
Hyattsville, MD 20782

Chrysler 300 Club Int'l
19 Donegal Court
Ann Arbor, MI 48104

Chrysler 300 Club, Inc.
P.O. Box 6613
Texarkana, TX 75501

Club Dodge
P.O. Box 2493
Dearborn, MI 48123

Dart/Valiant Slant 6 Club of
Amer.
P.O. Box 1012
Lafayette, CA 94549

Daytona-Superbird Club
13717 W. Green Meadow Dr.
New Berlin, WI 53151

T/A AAR Special Interest Auto
Club
P.O. Box 30022
Columbus, OH 43230

DeSoto Club of America
105 E. 96th
Kansas City, MO 64114

Dodge Brothers Club
8621 Campus Dr.
Hayattsville, MD 20783

Dodge Wayfarer Sportabout
Registry
10905 Ft. Washington Road £102
Ft. Washington, MD 20744

Imperial Owners Club
P.O. Box 991
Scranton, PA 18503

Mo-Par Trans Am. Assoc.
525 Nashua Rd.
Liberty, MO 64068

Mopar Muscle Club
P.O. Box 368R
Lockport, IL 60441

National Chrysler Products Club
2119 Duncan Avenue
Allison Park, PA 15101

National Hemi Owners Assoc.
137 North View Road
Blanchester, OH 45107

Plymouth Barracuda/Cuda
Owners Club
16 Brentwood Drive
Peabody, MA 01960

Plymouth 4 & 6 Cyl.
203 Main St. E.
Cavalier, ND 58220

Scat Pack Club
P.O. Box 2303
Dearborn, MI 48123

Special Interest Auto Club
P.O. Box 30022
Columbus, OH 43230

Town & Country Owners Registry
406 W. 34th St.
Kansas City, MO 64111

Walter P. Chrysler Club
Box 4705
No. Hollywood, CA 91607

DAF Club
19 Middleton Road
Greenport, NY 11944

Davis Three-Wheeler Club of Am.
3435 S. Broadway
Englewood, CO 80110

Devin Register
Box 18
Nyack, NY 10960

DeSoto Club of America
105 E. 96th
Kansas City, MO 64114

Durant Family Register
2700 Timber Lane
Green Bay, WI 54303-5899

EDSEL MODELS

Edsel Owners Club, Inc.
517 NE 112 Ave.
Vancouver, WA 98664

International Edsel Club
P.O. Box 86
Polo, IL 61064

Edsel Restorers Group
30715 Nine Mile Road
Farmington Hills, MI 48024

Facel Vega Owners Club
1650 E. 104th Street
Los Angeles, CA 90002

FORD MODELS

Early Ford V-8 Club of Amer.
P.O. Box 2122
San Leandro, CA 94577

Fabulous Fifties Ford Club
P.O. Box 286
Riverside, CA 92502

Ford Galaxie Club of America
1014 Chestnut St.,
P.O. Box 2206
Bremerton, WA 98310

Fairlane Club of America
721 Drexel Ave.
Drexel Hill, PA 19026

Ford-Mercury Club of Amer.
P.O. Box 3551
Hayward, CA 94540

Ford-Mercury Restorers Club
P.O. Box 2133
Dearborn, MI 48123

The Falcon Club of Amer.
P.O. Box 113
Jacksonville, AR 72076

Special Interest Fords of the '50s
5007 Wedgewood
Bellaire, TX 77401

Crown Victoria Assoc.
Rt. 5
Bryan, OH 43506

International Ford Retractable
  Club
P.O. Box 92
Jerseyville, IL 62052

Model T Ford Club of Amer.
Box 7400
Burbank, CA 91510-7400

Model T Ford Club Int'l
P.O. Box 915
Elgin, IL 60120

Model A Ford Club of America
P.O. Box 250 S. Cypress
La Habra, CA 90631

Model A Drivers Inc.
1804 DeGrand St.
Green Bay, WI 54304

Model A Restorers Club
24822 Michigan Ave.
Dearborn, MI 48121

Model A Cabriolet Club
6406 Glenbard Road
Burke, VA 22015

The Mustang Club of Amer.
P.O. Box 447
Lithonia, GA 30058

Mustang Owners Club
2829 Cagua Dr. N.E.
Albuquerque, NM 87110

'71 429 Mustang Registry
P.O. Box 1472
Fair Oaks, CA 95628

Ranchero Club of America
1339 Beverly Rd.
Port Vue, PA 15133

Nifty Fifties Ford Club
P.O. Box 142
Macedonia, OH 44056

Classic T-Bird Club Int'l
P.O. Box 2398
10315 Jefferson Blvd.
Culver City, CA 90230

Vintage T-Bird Club of Amer.
P.O. Box 2250
Dearborn, MI 48123

Meteor Car Club
General Delivery
Bowmanville
Ontario, Canada L1C 3K1

Mustang & Classic Ford Club
P.O. Box 963
North Attleboro, MA 02761

Thunderbirds of Amer.
Box 2766
Cedar Rapids, IA 52406

Performance Ford Club of Amer.
P.O. Box 32
Asheville, OH 43103

Ford Sidevalve Owners Club
Box 491
Toughkenamon, PA 19374

Associated Fords of the '50s
P.O. Box 66161
Portland, OR 97226

H. W. Franklin Club
Cazenovia College
Cazenovia, NY 13035

Glas Owners Club
717 Spring Valley Pkwy.
Elko, NV 89801

Graham Owners Club
447 Fremont St.
Lancaster, PA 17603

Heinkle-Messerschmitt-Isetta
  Club
P.O. Box 90
Topanga, CA 90290

Hispano-Suiza Society
P.O. Box 688
Hayward, CA 94543

Hudson-Essex-Terraplane Club
100 E. Cross St.
Ypsilanti, MI 48197

Hupmobile Club Inc.
6820 Burma Road
Folsom, CA 95630

Impulse Int'l Auto Club
Box 2327
San Anselmo, CA 94960

Isotta Fraschini Owners Assoc.
35 Ligonier Drive, NE
North Fort Myers, FL 33903

Assoc. of Jensen Owners
1621 Palomino Lane
Kingwood, TX 77339

Jewett Owners Club
24005 Clawiter Road
Hayward, CA 94545

Jordan Register
58 Bradford Blvd.
Yonkers, NY 10710

Kaiser-Frazer Owners Club
P.O. Box 99
Norton, KS 67654-0099

King Midget & Eshelman
  Registry
50 Oakwood Drive
Ringwood, NJ 07456

Kissel Kar Klub
147 N. Rural St.
P.O. Box 305
Hartford, WI 53027

Knight-Overland Registry
2765 Joel Place, NE
Atlanta, GA 30360

Kurtis Kraft Register
Drawer 220
Oneonta, NY 13820

Lagonda Club
68 Savill Road
Lindfield, Haywards Heath
Sussex RH16 2NN England

LINCOLN MODELS

Lincoln Owner's Club
821 West Chicago St.
Algonquin, IL 60102

Lincoln-Zephyr Owners Club
2107 Steimruck Road
Elizabethtown, PA 17022

Continental MKII Owners Ass'n
17230 Oldenberg Road
Apple Valley, CA 92307

Road Race Lincoln Register
P.O. Box 2402
Seal Beach, CA 90740

56-57 Lincoln Registry
Box 10075
Elmwood, CT 06110

Lincoln-Cont. Owners Club
P.O. Box 549
Nogales, AZ 85621

Linc. Cosmopolitan Union
2914 Gulford
Royal Oak, MI 48073

Lincoln Cosmopolitan Owners
   Registry
2027 Ascot Dr.
Apt. No. 1
Moraga, CA 94556

MERCURY MODELS

The Mercury Club
702 Center Street
McKeesport, PA 15132

Cougar Club of America
1526 Ericson Pl.
Bronx, NY 10461

Mid-Century Mercury Car Club
5707 35th Ave.
Kenosha, WI 53142

Comet Enthusiasts Group
2520 Homewood Place
White Bear Lake, MN 55110

Cougar Eliminator Union
2914 Gulford
Royal Oak, MI 48073

NASH (& METRO. Also see AMC)

Nash Car Club of Amer.
Rt. 1, Box 253
Clinton, IA 52732

Nash-Healey Car Club
530 Edgewood Ave.
Trafford, PA 15085

Metropolitan Club
Box 2951 New River Stage
Phoenix, AZ 85029

Metro Owners Club of NA
839 W. Race Street
Somerset, PA 15301

Nash Metropolitan Club
2244 Cross St.
LaCanada, CA 91011

Metropolitan Owners Club
49 Carleton
Westbury, NY 11590

NSU Enthusiasts USA
P.O. Box 1281
Farmington, NM 87401

OLDSMOBILE MODELS

57 Oldsmobile Chapter
151 Rivera Ct.
Chula Vista, CA 92011

Hurst/Olds Club of Amer.
3623 Burchfield
Lansing, MI 48901

Oldsmobile Performance
45 Rochelle Ave.
Rochelle Park, NJ 07662

Oldsmobile Club of America
P.O. Box 16216
Lansing, MI 48901

Curved Dash Olds Club
P.O. Box 16
Bremo Bluff, VA 23022

National Antique Oldsmobile
   Club
P.O. Box 483
Elmont, NY 11003

Opel USA
64 Eaton Road
Tolland, CT 06084

PACKARD MODELS

Packards Int'l Motor Car Club
302 French St.
Santa Ana, CA 92701

The Packard Club
Packard Auto Classics, Inc.
P.O. Box 2808
Oakland, CA 94618

The Packard Caribbean Roster
P.O. Box 765
Huntington Beach, CA 92648

Packard Truck Organization
RD 1, Box 256
York Springs, PA 17372

Packard V-8 Roster, '55-'56
7050 Owensmouth Ave.
Canoga Park, CA 91303

PONTIAC MODELS

Pontiac Oakland Club Int'l
P.O. Box 4789
Culver City, CA 90230

Classic G.T.O. Club
P.O. Box 392
Dallas, TX 75221

G.T.O. Ass'n of Amer.
1634 Briarson
Saginaw, MI 48604

Oakland-Pontiac Enthusiasts
Organ.
1083 Woodlow Street
Pontiac, MI 48054

Trans AM Club
P.O. Box 917
Champaign, IL 61820

Trans AM Club of America
P.O. Box 33085
North Royalton, OH 44133

Trans AM Club U.S.A.
Box 99
Medford, MA 02153

Judge GTO International
114 Prince George Drive
Hampton, VA 23669

Original GTO Club, Int'l
P.O. Box 18483
Milwaukee, WI 53218

Fiero Owners Club of America
1941 E. Edinger Ave.
Santa Ana, CA 92705

National Fiero Owners Assoc.
176 Edgebrook Road
Robbinsville, NJ 08691

No. Amer. Singer Owners Club
6176 Caleta
Goleta, CA 93117

Stevens-Duryea Assoc.
3565 Newhaven Road
Pasadena, CA 91107

Stevens Owners Registry
401 Brokker Road
Brandon, FL 33511

STUDEBAKER MODELS

Erkine Register
441 E. St. Clair.
Almont, MI 48003

Antique Studebaker Club
4476 Matilija Avenue
Sherman Oaks, CA 91423

Studebaker Drivers Club
8330 Moberly Lane
Dallas, TX 75227

Studebaker Auto Club of Amer.
P.O. Box 5036
Hemet, CA 92343

Avanti Owners Association Int'l
P.O. Box 296
Westminster, CO 80030

Tucker Club of America
982 Doerner Rd.
Roseburg, OR 97470

TVR Car Club
4450 S. Park Ave.
Apt. 1609
Chevy Chase, MD 20815

WILLS

The Wills Club
1604 James Road
Wantagh, NY 11793

Wills St. Claire Club
721 Jenkinson St.
Port Huron, MI 48060

WILLYS MODELS

Willys Overland Jeepster Club
Box 12042
El Paso, TX 79912

Midstates Jeepster Assoc.
7025 Lorraine Terrace
Stickney, IL 60402

The Willys Club
1850 Valley Forge Road
Landsdale, PA 19446

Willys Overland Knight Registry
241 Orchard Drive
Dayton, OH 45419

Willys-8 Registry
1415 Baker Street
Penticton, BC Canada
V2A 6B7

Woodill Wildfire Registry
826 Villa Ridge Road
Falls Church, VA 22046

RELATED ORGANIZATIONS

Amphibious Auto Club of
America
3281 Elk Court
Yorktown Heights, NY 10598

Automobile License Plate
Collectors Assoc.
P.O. Box 712
Weston, WV 26452

Automobile Objects d'art Club
252 N. 7th Street
Allentown, PA 18102

British Motorcar Club
BIR-106
Rocky Hill, CT 06067

Canadian Street Rod Assoc.
604 River Road South
Peterborough, Ont. Canada K9J
1E7

Electric Auto Assoc.
1249 Lane Street
Belmont, CA 94002

Fordson Tractor Club
250 Robinson Road
Cave Junction, OR 97532

Hubcap Collectors Club Int'l
Box 54
Buckley, MI 49620

Key Chain Collectors Club
888 8th Ave.
New York, NY 10019

Madison Ave. Sports Car Driving
& Chowder Society
30 Sumner Road
Greenwich, CT 06830

Micro Car Club
5220 Brittany Drive S. £1406
St. Petersburg, FL 33715

Mullins Owners Club
1427 W. Idaho Ave.
St. Paul, MN 55108

Pace Car Society
1490 Overhill Road
Golden, CO 80401

Pioneer Machinery Club
RR 4
LeMars, IA 51031

Registry of Italian Oddities
3205 Valley Vista Road
Walnut Creek, CA 94598

Sedan Deliveries of Calif.
P.O. Box 1265
Vista, CA 92083

Society of Automotive Historians
Automotive History Collection
Detroit Public Library
5201 Woodward Ave.
Detroit, MI 48202

Steam Auto Club of Amer.
1227 W. Voorhees St.
Danville, IL 61832

U.S.A. Convertible Club
P.O. Box 8240
Cincinnati, OH 45208

TOYS AND MODELS

Ertl Collector's Club
Dept. 776A
Hwys 136 & 20
Dyersville, IA 52040

Matchbox Collectors Club
P.O. Box 119
Woodridge, NJ 07075

Model Car Collectors Ass'n
5113 Sugar Leaf Dr.
Roanoke, VA 24018

STATION WAGONS

National Woodie Club
5522 West 140th St.
Hawthorne, CA 90250

TRUCK CLUBS

Amer. Truck Hist. Society
Saunders Building
201 Office Park Dr.
Birmingham, AL 35223

Antique Truck Club of Amer.
P.O. Box 291
Hershey, PA 17033

Military Vehicle Collectors
P.O. Box 2282
Charlotte, NC 28211

Light Commercial Vehicle Ass'n
Rt 14, Box 468
Jonesboro, TN 37659

National Chevy/GMC Truckin'
Club
P.O. Box 119
Santa Barbara, CA 93102

Int'l Harvester Restorers Club
P.O. Box 2281
Elkhart, IN 46516

Graham Bros. Truck & Bus Club
9894 Fairtree Drive
Stongsville, OH 44136

Diamond T Register
P.O. Box 1657
St. Cloud, MN 56302

Nat'l Panel Del'y Club
4002½ Hermitage Rd.
Richmond, VA 23227

Motor Truck, Bus & Fire Engine
Club
330 N. Edwards Ave.
Syracuse, NY 13206

Vintage White Truck Assoc.
629 Terminal Way £21
Costa Mesa, CA 92627

Ultra Van
1199 Dunsyre Dr.
Lafayette, CA 94549

State-by-State Car Club Listing

ALABAMA

Gadsden Antique Auto Club
113 Buckingham Pl.
Gadsden, AL 35901

Old South Antique Auto Club
Rt. 9, Box 72B
Eight Mile, AL 36613

ARKANSAS

Arkansas Antique Car Club
610 S. 12th St.
Paragould, AR 72450

Arkansas Traveler Antique Auto
Club
7521 Gable Dr.
Little Rock, AR 72205

Bootheel Antique Car Club
562 N. 7th St.
Piggott, AR 72454

Dixie Car Club
P.O. Box 1255
Benton, AR 72015

Foothills of the Ozarks Antique
Car Club
Rt. 1 Box 212
Rogers, AR 72756

Fort Smith Antique Automobile
Club
3301 South 95th
Fort Smith, AR 72903

Mid-America Old Time
Automobile Association
Museum of Automobiles
Rt. 3, Petit Jean Mtn.
Morrilton, AR 72110

Razorback Antique Auto Club
Rt. 1, Box 796
Heber Springs, AR 72543

Valley Antique Automobile Club
704 Ave. 2 NE
Atkins, AR 72823

Vintage and Classic Cars of Hot
Springs
907 Prospect
Hot Springs, AR 71901

ARIZONA

Arizona Edsel Club
8324 East Via Dorado
Scottsdale, AZ 85258

Arizona MGT Roadrunners
P.O. Box 246
Temple, AZ 85281

Cactus Corvair Club
P.O. Box 11471
Phoenix, AZ 85061

The Early Ford V-8 Club
Phoenix Chapter
1502 W. 1st Pl.
Mesa, AZ 85201

Ford Falcon Club of Ariz.
10209 N. 64 St.
Scottsdale, AZ 85253

Packards International Arizona
Region
3008 E. Cheery Lynn Rd.
Phoenix, AZ 85016

CALIFORNIA

American Truck Historical Society
Central California Chapter
6412 East Keyes Rd.
Turlock, CA 95380

Antique Automobile Club of
America
Redwood Empire Region
P.O. Box 3901
Santa Rosa, CA 95402

Arcane Auto Society
875 Folsom St.
San Francisco, CA 94107

Association of Calif. Car Clubs
827 Fourth St. #208
Santa Monica, CA 90403

Austin-Healey Club
Pacific Centre, P.O. Box 6197
San Jose, CA 95150

Avanti Owner Ass'n Int'l
San Diego Chapter
7840 Michelle Dr.
La Mesa. CA 92041

California Assoc. of Tiger Owners
4508 El Reposo Dr.
Eagle Rock, CA 90065

California Capri Club
422 Bradrick
San Leandro, CA 94578

California MGT Register
4911 Winnetka Ave.
Woodland Hills, CA 91364

California Vehicle Foundation
5240 Fruitridge Rd.
Sacramento, CA 95820

Central Calif. MoPar Association
P.O. Box 5659
Stockton, CA 95205

Central Cast Triumphs
718 "D" W. Victoria
Santa Barbara, CA 93101

Classic Car Club of America
Southern California Region
4913 Biloxi Ave.
North Hollywood, CA 91601

Contemporary Historical Vehicle
  Association
Costal Galleys Region
P.O. Box 2194
Canoga Park, CA 91306

Contemporary Historical Vehicle
  Association
Redwood Region
3253 La Canada Rd.
Lafayette, CA 94549

Corsa West of Los Angeles
P.O. Box 5023
Mission Hills, CA 91345

Desert Tin of Southern California
P.O. Box 329
Sunnymead, CA 92388

Early Ford V-8 Club
San Diego Region
Box 715
La Mesa, CA 92041

Falcon Club of Los Angeles
P.O. Box 5694
Elmonte, CA 91734

Ford Falcon Club of San Diego
P.O. Box 33306
San Diego, CA 92103

Ford-Mercury Club of America
Cable Car Chapter
22588 7th St.
Hayward, CA 94541

Ford-Mercury Club of America
Mid-Atlantic Chapter
3616 Woodburn Rd.
Annandale, CA 22003

Ford-Mercury Club of America
San Fernando Valley Chapter
22706 Catley St.
Canogo Park, CA 91367

Ford-Mercury Club of America
San Gabriel Valley Chapter
P.O. Box 943
Baldwin Park, CA 91706

Horseless Carriage Club of
  Southern California
4527 Yosemite Way
Los Angeles, CA 90065

Hudson-Essex-Terraplane Club
California Inland Chapter
15808 Glazebrook Dr.
La Mirada, CA 90638

Hudson-Essex-Terraplane Club
Northern California Chapter
P.O. Box 2454
Berkeley, CA 94702

Kaiser-Frazer Owners Club
  International
Southern California Region
3248 Washington Place
La Crescenta, CA 91214

Last of the Thirties Club
P.O. Box 1
Manteca, CA 95336

Long Beach Model T Club
P.O. Box 7112
Long Beach, CA 90807

Mustang Club of Southern
  California
15168 Ashwood Lane
Chino, CA 91710

Mustang Owners Club of
  California
P.O. Box 6454
Thousand Oaks, CA 91359

Nash Club of America
Southern California Region
2428 Level St.
Anaheim, CA 92804

Northern California Chrysler
  Products Club
11271 Fardon Ave.
Los Altos, CA 94022

Northern Calif. Kit Car Club
60 Rider Court
Walnut Creek, CA 94595

Northern California Packards
P.O. Box 7763
Fremont, CA 94537

North Valley Unique Car Club
988 Ellene Ave.
Chico, CA 95926

The 57 Oldsmobile Chapter
151 Riviera Ct.
Chula Vista, CA 92011

Orange County Model T Ford
  Club Inc.
1922 S. Anaheim Blvd.
Anaheim, CA 92805

Pacific Austin Bantam Club
12304 Lambert Avenue
El Monte, CA 91732

Pontiac Oakland Club
  International
Southern California Region
1307 Santanella Terrace
Corona del Mar, CA 92625

Renault Club of Southern
  California
1516 East Santa Ana St.
Anaheim, CA 92805

Sacramento Valley Citroen Club
3348 Ardenridge Dr.
Sacramento, CA 95825

San Diego MG Club
P.O. Box 112111
San Diego, CA 92111

South Bay AMX Club
1980 Kingman Ave.
San Jose, CA 95128

Southern California Willys
  Overland Jeepsters Club
5935 Harvey Way
Lakewood, CA 90713

Special Ts
P.O. Box 1778
Golita, CA 93116

Studebaker Drivers Club
Beach Cities Chapter
17th St. at Newport Freeway
Santa Ana, CA

Studebaker Drivers Club
Orange County Beach Cities
  Chapter
533 Catalina Dr.
Newport Beach, CA 92663

Triumph Travelers SCC
1658 Meadowlark
Sunnyvale, CA 94007

Vintage Chevrolet Club of
  America
Foothill Region
1751 E. Alosta Ave.
Glendora, CA 91740

Vintage Chevrolet Club of
  America
Sacramento Valley Region
8780 Golden Spur Dr.
Roseville, CA 95678

West Coast Kustoms
P.O. Box 329
Sunnymead, CA 92388

Western States Corvette Council
2321 Falling Water Court
Santa Clara, CA 95054

Willys Aero Survival Count
3248 Washington Pl.
LaCrescenta, CA 91214

COLORADO

Alfa Club of Colorado
11253 E. 6th Pl.
Aurora, CO 80010

Am. MGB Assoc. & Rocky Mtn.
  MGT Register
1218 Steele
Denver, CO 80206

Classic Chevys of Colorado
6621 Fielding Cr.
Colorado Springs, CO 80911

Classic GTO Association of
  Denver
6883 Wyman Way
Westminister, CO 80030

Coloradans
2000 W. 92nd Ave., #275
Federal Heights, CO 80221

Colorado Association of Tiger
  Owners
7939-2 York
Denver, CO 80229

Colorado Camaro Club
1164 Regina Lane
Northglenn, CO 80233

Colorado Classic Thunderbird
  Club
15 Flower St.
Lakewood, CO 80226

Colorado Continental Convertible
  Club
695 Dudley St.
Lakewood, CO 80226

Colorado Street Rod Association
12416 Bellaire
Thornton, CO 80241

Denver Coupe & Sedan
2755 W. 12th Ave. Pl.
Broomfield, CO 80020

Denver Mustang Club
5704 W. Leewood Dr.
Littleton, CO 80123

High Plains Nash
1974 S. Huron
Denver, CO 80223

Lotus-Colorado
7673 Beverly Blvd.
Castle Rock, CO 80104

Mile High Buick
47355 Galapaco
Englewood, CO 80110

Mile High Nomads
6208 W. 92nd Pl.
Westminster, CO 80030

Mile High Skyliners
750 S. Brianwood Dr.
Lakewood, CO 80226

Model A Denver
1082 S. Harrison
Denver, CO 80209

Model A Pikes Peak
8180 Piute Rd.
Colorado Springs, CO 80903

Pikes Peak Corvair
205 N. El Paso St.
Colorado Springs, CO 80903

Porsche Club of America
Rocky Mountain Region
10 Brookside Dr.
Littleton, CO 80121

Rocky Mountain Classic Chevys
P.O. Box 1125
Idaho Springs, CO 80452

Rocky Mountain Corsa
9753 W. Virginia Dr.
Lakewood, CO 80226

Rocky Mountain Isetta Club
6516 Constellation Dr.
Fort Collins, CO 80525

Rocky Mountain Jaguar Club
1575 W. Byers Pl.
Denver, CO 80223

Rocky Mountain Military Vehicle
4675 Teller St.
Wheatridge, CO 80033

Rocky Mountain Packard
2920 Ward Ct.
Denver, CO 80033

Rocky Mountain Thunderbird
Club
2860 S. Kenton Ct.
Aurora, CO 80014

Rocky Mountain 1958-66
Thunderbird Club
451 E. 58th Avenue, No. 1185
Denver, CO 80216

Rocky Mt. UN-Club
1204 S. Uvalda
Aurora, CO 80012

Studebaker Drivers Club
Studebaker Conestoga
320 W. 80th Ave.
Denver, CO 80221

Thunderbirds of Colorado
Limited
10442 Brewer Dr.
Northglenn, CO 80234

Veteran Motor Car Club of
America
Loveland Chapter
2112 Champa St.
Loveland, CO 80537

Veteran Motor Car Club of
America
Arkansas Valley Chapter
439 Westwood Lane
Pueblo, CO 81005

Veteran Motor Car Club of
America
Royal Gorge Chapter
1411 Walnut
Canon City, CO 81212

Ye Old Auto Club
14706 E. 134th Pl
Brighton, CO 80601

Yesteryears Classics
9800 Lunceford Lane
Northglenn, CO 80221

CONNECTICUT

Connecticut Valley Willys
Overland Jeepster Club
15 Conrad Drive
W. Hartford, CT 06107

The Eastern Packard Club
P.O. Box 153
Fairfield, CT 06430

Historical Automobile Club
Litchfield Hills
31 Morningside Dr.
Torrington, CT 06790

New England Antique Racers Inc.
P.O. Box 18354
East Hartford, CT 06118

New England Street Rodders Inc.
75 Tolland Turnpike
Manchester, CT 06040

FLORIDA

Antique Automobile Club of
America
Florida West Coast Region
2871 County Rd. 70
Palm Harbor, FL 33563

Antique Auto Club of Cape
Canaveral
P.O. Box 1611
Cocoa, FL 32922

Contemporary Historical Vehicle
Association
Sunshine Region
2552 58th Ave. N.
St. Petersburg, FL 33714

Ford Lincoln Mercury Club of
Florida
P.O. Box 13514
Tampa, FL 33681

Gold Coast T-Bird Club
1675 NW 43rd St.
Oakland Park, FL 33309

Mercury Club of South Florida
4132 SW 22nd St.
Fort Lauderdale, FL 33317

Miami Corvette Association
249 Lafayette Drive
Miami Springs, FL 33166

Orlando Area Studebaker Club
P.O. Box 698
Altamone Springs, FL 32714

Panama City Classic and Antique
Car Association
P.O. Box 1962
Panama City, FL 32401

Pin-Mar Antique Club
P.O. Box 1235
Pinellas Park, FL 33565

Road Knights of South Florida
4132 SW 22nd St.
Fort Lauderdale, FL 33317

South Florida Corvairs
P.O. Box 895
Fort Lauderdale, FL 33302

Studebaker Drivers Club
Central Florida Chapter
96 Toddsmill Trace
Tarpon Springs, FL 33589

Studebaker Drivers Club
Orlando Area Chapter
P.O. Box 698
Alamonte Springs, FL 32714

GEORGIA

Buick Club of America
Dixie Chapter
241 Ithica Dr.
Marietta, GA 30067

Chrysler 300 Club
Md-South Chapter
Rt. 1, Box 119
Pendergrass, GA 30567

Corvair Atlanta
599 Inglewood Drive
Smyrna, GA 30080

ILLINOIS

American Motors Car Club
Heart of Illinois Chapter
RR1, Box 50
Brinfield, IL 61517

Antique Automobile Club of
America
Mississippi Valley Region
2047 32nd St.
Rock Island, IL 61201

Automobile Collectors Club of
the Greater Belleville (Ill.) Area
105 Van Rue Dr.
Belleville, IL 62221

Capri Club of Chicago
7158 W. Armitage
Chicago, IL 60635

Chicagoland Thunderbirds
1041 Rand
Villa Park, IL 60181

Corsa
Chicagoland Corvair Enthusiasts
519 E. Forest Ave.
West Chicago, IL 60185

Illinois Valley Olds Chapter
18650 South 76th Avenue
Tenley Park, IL 60477

John Bearce Ford Mustang Club
662 Knoll Crest Dr.
Peoria, IL 61614

Kane Kounty Kar Klub
302 Richards St.
Geneva, IL 60134

Late Great Chevy
Northern Illinois Chapter
800 Hayes Ct.
Harvard, IL 60033
815-943-7123

McLean County Antique Auto
Club
1340 E. Empire
Bloomington, IL 61701

Midwest Antique Classic
Motorcycle Club
721 S. Julian St.
Naperville, IL 60540

Mississippi Valley Historic Auto
Club
1108 N. 5th St.
Quincy, IL 62301

Model A Restorers Club
Illinois Region
4001 N. Denley
Schiller Park, IL 60176

Model A Restorers Club Inc.
Calumet Region
8817 S. Moody Ave.
Oak Lawn, IL 60453

Mustang Club of America
Southern Illinois Mustang Ass.
Alton, IL 62002

Northern Illinois Late Great
Chevys
800 Hayes Court
Harvard, IL 60033

Old Town Escorts Ltd. Model Car
Club
1933 N. Sedgwick St.
Chicago, IL 60614

Pontiac Oakland Club
International
Illinois Chapter
904 W. Parker Dr.
Schaumburg, IL 80194

Prairie Capital Corvair
Association
P.O. Box 954
Springfield, IL 62705

Quad Cities Cruisers
1411-31st St.
Rock Island, IL 61201

Rock River Restorers
P.O. Box 872
Rock Falls, IL 61071

Rods of Lincoln Land
2440 Nan St.
Aurora, IL 60504

Vintage Chevrolet Club of
America
Great Lakes Region
1258 Balmoral Ave.
Calumet City, IL 60409

Walter P. Chrysler Club
Northern Illinois Region
327 Highland Ave.
Elmhurst, IL 60126

Windy City Z Club
1419 Adams Street
Lake in the Hills, IL 60102

INDIANA

Antique & Classic Auto Club
4400 S. 9th St.
Terre Haute, IN 47802

Elkhart Vintage Auto Club
P.O. Box 489
Elkhart, IN 46415

Falcons Over Indiana
Rt. 4, Box 116
Alexandria, IN 46001

Hoosier Convertible Club
3434 E. 136th St.
Carmel, IN 46032

Indiana Street Rod Association
7046 Forest Park Dr.
Indianapolis, IN 46217

Lincoln Continental Owners Club
Hoosier Region
6416 Dean Rd.
Indianapolis, IN 46220

Michiana Antique Auto Club Inc.
910 State St.
LaPorte, IN 46350

Old Fort Model A Region
P.O. Box 13586
Fort Wayne, IN 46869

Packards International
Indiana Region
613 W. Orchard Lane
Greenwood, IN 46142

IOWA

Iowa Street Rodders Association
Box 6086
East Des Moines Station
Des Moines, IA 50309

Midstates Jeepster Association
3175 Kaufman Ave.
Dubuque, IA 52001

Northeast Iowa Classic Chevy
Club Inc.
P.O. Box 1206
Waterloo, IA 50704

Northern Iowa Association for
the Preservation & Restoration
of Antique Cars (N.I.A.P.R.A.)
1998 10th Ave. N.
Fort Dodge, IA 50501

North Iowa Vintage Auto Club
RR1
Mason City, IA 50401

Quad Cities Antique Ford Club
608 N. 8th Street
Eldridge, IA 52748

KANSAS

Contemporary Historical Vehicle
Association
Sunflower Region
1312 E. 15th St.
Lawrence, KS 66044

Midwest MGA Club
11731 W. 101st Street
Overland Park, KS 66214

Mo-Kan T-Bird Club
10505 Mohawk Lane
Leawood, KS 66206

Nifty-Fifties Classic Chevy Club
RR1, Box 19
Wakeeney, KS 67672

KENTUCKY

Ancient Age River City Street
Rods
2453 Eastway Dr.
Lexington, KY 40503

River City Street Rods
7507 Mallard Drive
Pleasure Ridge Park, KY 40258

LOUISANA

Ark-La-Tex Antique & Classic Car
Assoc.
P.O. Box 3353
Shreveport, LA 71103

GTO Association of America
Cabri D Acadienne (Louisiana)
Chapter
105 Cajun Street
Broussard, LA 70518

Cenla Old Car Club
P.O. Box 402
Alexandria, LA 71301

Florida Parishes Vintage Car Club
of Louisiana Inc.
P.O. Box 38
Ponchatoula, LA 70454

Mid-South Region Old Car Club
907 N. 35th St.
West Monroe, LA 71201

The Old Car Club of Baton
Rouge
3221 McConnell Dr.
Baton Rouge, LA 70809

Ruston Antique Car Club of LA
Rt. 3, Box 194B
Ruston, LA 71270

MARYLAND

Antique Automobile Club of
America
Eastern Shore Region
Box 144, 300 Corporation Rd.
Sharptown, MD 21861

Antique Club of Greater
Baltimore
208 Brightside Ave.
Pikesville, MD 21208

Convertible Owners Club of
Greater Baltimore
11311 Woodland Dr.
Timonium, MD 21093

Group Corvair
4008 Bedford Pl.
Suitland, MD 20746

GTO Association of America
The Royal GTOS (MD/VA/DC)
Chapters
441 Henryton S.
Laural, MD 20707

Southern Maryland Antique Auto
Club
P.O. Box 264
White Plains, MD 20695

Washington Volvo Club
5300 Yorktown Rd.
Bethesda, MD 20816

MASSACHUSETTS

Antique Truck Club of New
England
280 W. First Street
S. Boston, MA 02127

Bay State Antique Auto Club
Box 491
Norwood, MA 02062

Colonial Convair Club
40 Woodcrest Rd.
Boxford, MA 01921

Connecticut Valley Willys
Overland Jeepster Club
20 Colonial Ave.
Springfield, MA 01109

The Fall River Antique Auto Club
1751 Rodman St.
Fall River, MA 02721

Hudson-Essex-Terraplane Club
New England Chapter
12 Albert Rd.
Peabody, MA 01960

Massachusetts Antique Fire
Apparatus Association
P.O. Box 3332
Peabody, MA 01960

Massachusetts Street Rod
Association
10 Mohawk Dr.
Tewksbury, MA 01876

Model A Restorers Club of MA
Gilmore Hall
138 and Carver St.
Raynham, MA

Mustang & Classic Ford Club of
New England
P.O. Box 963
North Attleboro, MA 02761

New England Military Vehicles
Collectors Club
P.O. Box 907
Salem, MA 01970

New England Packard Motor Car
Club
76 Whipple Rd.
Billerica, MA 01821

Plymouth County Auto Club
P.O. Box 124
N. Plymouth, MA 02360

MICHIGAN

Classic Car Club of America
Michigan Region
13332 Winchester
Huntington Woods, MI 48070

Corsa
Detroit Area Chapter
267 Arizona
Rochester, MI 48063

Detroit Triumph Sportscar Club
13201 Common Rd.
Warren, MI 48093

Grand Rapids Antique Car Club
P.O. Box 1523
Grand Rapids, MI 49501

Horseless Carriage Club of
America
Grand Rapids Region
Grand Rapids Public Museum
54 Jefferson Ave. S.E.
Grand Rapids, MI

Kalamazoo Antique Auto
Restorers Club
7383 N. 12
Kalamazoo, MI 49009

Michigan License Plate
Collectors Association
2902 E. Pierson Road
Flint, MI 48506

Southwestern Michigan Car
Collectors
1734 Smyers Dr.
Benton Harbor, MI 49022

The Steam Automobile Club of
America Inc.
Box 285
Niles, MI 49120

Veteran Motor Car Club of
America
Great Lakes Region
5601 Hatchery Rd.
Drayton Plains, MI 48020

West Michigan Street Rod
Association
P.O. Box 4
Muskegon, MI 49443

MINNESOTA

Antique Automobile Club of
America
Central Chapter
8207 Clinton Ave. S.
Bloomington, MN 55420

Buick Club of America
Gopher State Chapter
P.O. Box 8964
Minneapolis, MN 55408

Chevy's Best
7527 Chicago Ave.
Richfield, MN 55423

The Early Ford V-8 Club of
    America
Twin Cities Regional Group
P.O. Box 20236
Minneapolis, MN 55420

Ford-Mercury Club of America
North Land Late Eight
1097 W. Iowa Ave.
St. Paul, MN 55117

GTO Association of America
Land of Lake GTOs (Minnesota)
1630 E. Sandhurst Drive
Maplewood, MN 55109

Minnesota Packard's
Packard Club Region
Box 19119, Diamond Lake Station
Minneapolis, MN 55419

Minnesota Street Rod
    Association
4045 Hodgson Rd., Apt. 123
Shoreview, MN 55112

Model A Restorers Club
Twin Cities Model A Chapter
2712 Murray Ave. NE
Minneapolis, MN 55418

North Suburban Auto
    Enthusiasts
13064 Talor St. NE
Blaine, MN 55434

Pontiac-Oakland Club
    International
Tomahawk Chapter
2325 NE Taft St.
Minneapolis, MN 55418

Red River Wheelers
P.O. Box 332
Crookston, MN 56716

St. Cloud Antique Auto Club
P.O. Box 704
St. Cloud, MN 56302

Stephen Auto Club
RR1, Box 103
Stephen, MN 56757

Studebaker Drivers Club
Minn. Region (includes North
    Star & North Land Wheels)
P.O. Box 1004
Duluth, MN 55810

'T' Totalers of Minnesota
Model T Ford Club International
5319 Minnehaha Ave. So.
Minneapolis, MN 55417

Valley Vintage
Rt. 1, Box 48
Hawley, MN 56549

Vintage Car Club
922 Lincoln Ave, East
Alexandria, MN 56308

Vintage Chevrolet Club of
    America
Viking Region
Rt. 1, Box 75A
Buffalo, MN 55313

MISSISSIPPI

Antique Automobile & Engine
    Club of Mississippi
Gulf Hills Inn
Ocean Springs, MS 39564

Antique Vehicle Club of
    Mississippi
Box 347
Flora, MS 39071

Bear Creek Collector's Car Club
Box 773
Belmont, MS 38827

Cadillac Club
507 E. Walnut
Ripley, MS 38663

Mid-America Old Time Auto
    Association
323 Enchanted Dr.
Vicksburg, MS 39180

Mississippi Antique Car Club
604 Racove Dr.
Tupelo, MS 38801

Mississippi Model A Ford
    Restorers Club
1601 Twin Oak Dr.
Clinton, MS 39056

Oxford Antique Motorcar
    Association
1413 So. 10th St.
Oxford, MS 38655

Pine Belt Antique Automobile
    Club, Inc.
200 Robin Dr.
Petal, MS 39465 (Hattiesburg)

Studebaker Drivers Club
Central Mississippi Chapter
1313 Crawford
Vicksburg, MS 39180

Vintage Wheels, Meridian,
    Mississippi
1517 57th Court
Meridian, MS 39301

MISSOURI

Ford-Mercury Club of America
Gateway Chapter
P.O. Box 6641
St. Louis, MO 63125

GTO Association of America
Gateway GTO Association (MK/IL)
2161 Yale, Apt. 3
St. Louis, MO 63143

The Horseless Carriage Club of
  Missouri Inc.
226 Henry Ave.
Manchester, MO 63011

KC Kustoms
P.O. Box 1613
Independence, MO 64005

Metro Antique Auto Club
5308 Phelps Rd.
Kansas City, MO 64136

Midwest MGA Club
816 Wyandotte
Kansas City, MO 64105

Mississippi Valley Packards
602 S. Franklin
Farmington, MO 63640

Ozark Antique Auto Club
214 Jackson Road
Republic, MO 65738

Rod-Tiques
P.O. Box 1942
Independence, MO 64055

Studebaker Drivers Club
Missouri/Illinois ''Gateway''
  Chapter
701 Kehrs Mill Rd.
Ballwin, MO 63011

MONTANA

Treasure State Classics
817 Edith
Missoula, MT 59801

NEBRASKA

Classic Thunderbird Club of
  Omaha
1802 S. 76th Ave.
Omaha, NE 68124

Goldenrod Antique Car Club
1605 Avenue C
Cozad, NE 69130

Meadowlark Model A Club Inc.
P.O. Box 6011
Omaha, NE 68106

Mid-West Street Rod Association
P.O. Box 3705
Omaha, NE 68103

Mustang Car Club of Omaha
1835 N. 49 Ave.
Omaha, NE 68104

Nebraskaland Model T and
  Antique Car Club
2221 S. 37th
Lincoln, NE 68506

Nebraskaland Thunderbird Club
  Inc.
7922 Himebaugh Ave.
Omaha, NE 68134

Studebaker Drivers Club
Buffalo Bill Chapter
223 Reid
North Platte, NE 69101

Vintage Chevrolet Club of
  America
Eastern Neb./Western Iowa
2555 S. 125 Ave.
Omaha, NE 68144

Vintage Chevrolet Club of
  America
Tower of the Plains Region
Box 552
Milford, NE 68405

NEW HAMPSHIRE

New England Sonett Club
P.O. Box 4362
Manchester, NH 03108

NEW JERSEY

Bayshore Corvair Association
P.O. Box 815
Jackson, NJ 08527

Buick Club of America
Jersey Shore Buick
2425 Cedar St.
Manasquan, NJ 08736

Central Jersey Mustang Club
P.O. Box 354
Pennington, NJ 08534

Garden State Classic T-Bird Club
965 Swenlin Dr.
Vineland, NJ 08360

Jersey Late Greats '58-'64 Chevys
P.O. Box 1294
Hightstown, NJ 08520

The Lagonda Club
10 Crestwood Trail, Lake Mohawk
Sparta, NJ 07871

Model A Ford Club Inc.
Delaware Valley
Cherry Hill, NJ 08002

New Chervolet Club Formed in
  New Jersey
52 Colson Ave
Trenton, NJ 08610

North Jersey Thunderbird
  Association
8 Stag Trail
Fairfield, NJ 07006

Restored Rusty Relics
189 Marcotte Lane
Bergenfield, NJ 07621

Studebaker Drivers Club
Garden State Chapter
181 Villa Place
Rahway, NJ 07065

Triumph Association
North New Jersey Chapter
15 Northwood Ave., Apt. A-8
Summit, NJ 07901

Vintage Triumph Register
Detroit Triumph SCC
13201 Common
Warren, NJ 07060

NEW YORK

Antique Automobile Club of
America
Lake Erie Region
Pin Oak Dr.
Williamville, NY 14221

Antique Automobile Club of
America
Staten Island Region
Box 244 GPO
Staten Island, NY 10314

Automobilists of the Upper
Hudson Valley
Apt. A-13 Village One Apt.
587 Bdwy
Menands, NY 12204

Contemporary Historical Vehicle
Association
Big Apple Region
73-17 68 Rd.
Middle Village, NY 11379

Crosley Auto Club Inc.
3323 Eaton Rd.
Williamson, NY 14589

Early Ford V8 Club
Long Island Regional Club
23 Fairview Avenue
Valley Stream, NY 11581

Hudson Valley Classic Chevy
Club
Richard M. Warner
22 Pellbridge Dr.
Hopewell Junction, NY 12533

H. W. Franklin Club
Cazenovia College
Cazenovia, NY 13035

Long Island Chevy Owners
Association
19 Twin Lane N.
Wantagh, NY 11793

Long Island Ford-Mercury Club
P.O. Box 336
Ronkonkoma, NY 11779

The New England "T" Register,
LTS.
Drawer 220
Oneonta, NY 13820

Oldsmobile Performance
45 Rochelle Ave.
Rochelle Park, NJ 07662

Thunderbird Owners of New York
127 Ocean Ct.
Massapequa, NY 11758

Vintage Chevrolet Club of
America
Long Island Region
27 Ashwood Ct.
East Northport, NY 11731

NORTH CAROLINA

Austin-Healey Club
Triad Area
P.O. Box 5640
Winston-Salem, NC 27113

Carolina Mountain Rods &
Classics
P.O. Box 1644
Hendersonville, NC 28739

OHIO

Antique Automobile Club of
America
Central Chapter of Ohio Region
8166 Brownsville Road S.E.
Glenford, OH 43739

Buckeye Motorcar Association
P.O. Box 128
Newark, OH 43055

Buick Club of America
Central Ohio Chapter
90 E. Cherry St.
Sunbury, OH 43074

Central Ohio Buick Club
115 Glenmont Ave.
Columbus, OH 43214

Citroen Car Club of Ohio
38570 Butcher Rd.
Leetonia, OH 44431

Friends of the Crawford Auto-
Aviation Museum
P.O. Box 751
Willoughby, OH 44094

The Great Lakes Roadster Club
P.O. Box 302
Bath, OH 44210

Jaguar Club of Ohio
2874 Chadbourne Road
Shaker Heights, OH 44120

Lancaster Old Car Club
P.O. Box 322
Lancaster, OH 43130

Mahoning Valley Olde Car Club
Inc.
623 N. Hartford Ave.
Youngstown, OH 44509

Massillon Area Car Club
7981 Windward NW
Massillon, OH 44646

Ohio Chrysler Products Antique
Auto Club
5198 Harmony Lane
Willoughby, OH 44094

Packards International
Midwest Region
365 St. Leger Ave.
Akron, OH 44305

Penn-Ohio Model A Ford Club
139 East Main Street
Shelby, OH 44875

Street Survivors Car Club
745 County Line Road
Hopewell, OH 43746

Tri-State F-100 (53-56)
128 West 72nd Street
Cincinnati, OH 45016

United States Camaro Club
P.O. Box 24489
Huber Heights, OH 45424

Valley Street Rodders
P.O. Box 1000
Millfield, OH 45761

Vintage Vettes of Cincy
5868 N. Highwood
Fairfield, OH 45014

Y-City Custom Car Association
2090 Shady Lane
Zanesville, OH 43701

OKLAHOMA

C. A. R. S. Unlimited of Western
Oklahoma
P.O. Box 2845
Elk City, OK 73648

GTO Association of America
Goats of Northeastern Oklahoma
Chapter
1200 W. Austianks, OK 97106

OREGON

Classic AMX Club of Eugene
P.O. Box 8162
Coburg, OR 97401

Ford-Mercury Club of America
Santiam Chapter
2932 Hill SE
Albany, OR 97321

Ford-Mercury Club of America
Sunset Chapter
P.O. Box 254
Banks, OR 97106

Goat Herd GTO Club of Oregon
P.O. Box 23924
Portland, OR 97223

Pacific NW Convertible Club
P.O. Box 16511
Portland, OR 97216

Till-A-Wheels Multi-Marque
P.O. Box 461
Tillamook, OR 97141

PENNSYLVANIA

Antique Automobile Club of
America
Pottstown Region
951 N. 12th St.
Reading, PA 19604

1953-54 Buick Skylark Registry
737 St. Claire Ave.
Erie, PA 16505

Central PA Corvair Club
1751 Chesley Road
York, PA 17403

Fairlane Club of America
721 Drexel Ave.
Drexel Hill, PA 19026

GTO Association of America
Northeastern GTOs
98 Regent St.
Wilkes-Barre, PA 18702

Lambda Car Club
1944 South St.
Philadelphia, PA 19146

Lehigh Valley Model "A" Club
P.O. Box 9031
Bethlehem, PA 18018-9031

Mercedes-Benz Club of Northeast
Pa.
229 Cedar Street
Allentown, PA 18102

The Mercury Club
702 Center St.
McKeesport, PA 15132

Model A Restorers Club
Delaware Valley Region
4215 Howell St.
Philadelphia, PA 19135

Mustang Club of America
First Pennsylvania Mustang Club
Chapter
610 Fitch Rd.
Hatboro, PA 19040

Northeast Hemi Owners
Association
681 Black Road
Bryn Mawr, PA 19010

Pontiac Owners Club
International
Keystone Chapter
9 Top-of-the-Oaks
Chadds Ford, PA 19317

Quaker City Citroen Car Club
307 Summit Ave.
Fort Washington, PA 19034

The Ranchero Club
1339 Beverly Road
Port Vue, PA 15133

Tigers East/Alpines East
P.O. Box 1260
Kulpsville, PA 19443

Studebaker Drivers Club
Keystone Region
Rd. 1357
Bethel, PA 19507

Union Historical Fire Society
1307 N. 19th
Allentown, PA 18104

Willys Club
509 W. Germantown Pike
Norristown, PA 19403

The Worthington Register
1918/1938 T, A & B Tractors
Rd. 2, Box 44
Mertztown, PA 19539

RHODE ISLAND

Cadillac-LaSalle Club Inc.
New England Region
160 Edgewood Blvd.
Providence, RI 02905

Mustang Car Club of New
  England
Box 1554
Woonsocket, RI 02895

Rhode Island Vintage Wheels
12 Austin St.
Wakefield, RI 02879

SOUTH CAROLINA

Camaros of Columbia
39 East Fern Ct.
Columbia, SC 29210

SOUTH DAKOTA

Dakota Territories Model A Club
Sioux Falls, SD 57101

TENNESSEE

Forked Deer Antique Car Club
2511 E. Count St.
Dyersburg, TN 38024

Magnolia Antique Car Club
Rt. 2, Box 139
Michie, TN 38357

Memphis Old Time Car Club
1749 Graceland Cove
Memphis, TN 38116

Tennessee Valley Automobile
  Club
P.O. Box 116
Paris, TN 38242

West Tennessee Antique Car
  Club
44 Grassland Dr.
Jackson, TN 38301

TEXAS

Amarillo Antique Car Club
203 E. Hastings
Amarillo, TX 79108

Antique Automobile Club of
  America
Golden Triangle Chapter
98 Orgain
Beaumont, TX 77707

Antique Automobile Club of
  America
Texas Region
1431 Ridgeview St.
Mesquite, TX 75149

Austin Area Street Machines
  Association
Rt. 2, Box 51-A
Manor, TX 78653

Austin-Healey Club of America
South Texas Region
1800 San Pedro
San Antonio, TX 78212

Corvette Owners Association of
  South Texas
Rt. 1, Box 119-B
4080 Menger Road
Wetmore, TX 78163

Early Ford V8 Club of America
Southern Texas Regional Group
4438 Newport Woods
San Antonio, TX 78249

Early Ford V-8
Golden Spread Region
Box 1782
Amarillo, TX 79105

El Rey De La Tierra Mojada
5757 Alpha Road, #201
Dallas, TX 75240

Ford-Mercury Club of America
Longhorn Late Eight
10905 Scotsmeadow
Dallas, TX 75218

GTO Association of America
Lone Star GTO Club Chapter
1105 Floradale Drive
Austin, TX 78753

Lone Star Edsel Club
2209 B. Chasewych
Austin, TX 78745

Piney Wood As
P.O. Box 7855
The Woodlands, TX 77387

Porsche Club of America
Long Horn Region Inc.
4426 Newport Woods
San Antonio, TX 78249

North San Antonio Street
  Machines
120 Wagon Trail
San Antonio, TX 78231

Packards International
Texas Region
359 Sussex
San Antonio, TX 78221

Pontiac-Oakland International
South Central Texas Chapter
3023 Clearfield
San Antonio, TX 78230

San Antonio Classic Thunderbird
Club
607 Jackson Keller
San Antonio, TX 78216

San Antonio Mustang Club
12118 Ridge Spur
San Antonio, TX 78247

San Antonio Street Rods
3901 S. Presa
San Antonio, TX 78210

South Texas Four Wheelers
7350 Nickle
San Antonio, TX 78249

South Texas Triumphs
6710 Country Breeze
San Antonio, TX 78240

Texas Corvette Association
1806 Oak Mountain
San Antonio, TX 78232

UTAH

Ford-Mercury Club of America
Rocky Mountain Chapter
2926 Banbury Rd.
Salt Lake City, UT 84121

VIRGINIA

Antique Automobile Club of
America
Tidewater Region
5500 Elizabeth Ave.
Norfolk, VA 23502

Antique Automobile Club of
America
Tri-County Region
Rt. 1, Box 91
Linville, VA 22834

GTO Association of America
Greater Tidewater Owners
Society (GTOS)
3632 Starlighter Drive
Virginia Beach, VA 23452

Model A Ford Cabriolet Club
6406 Glenbard Road
Burke, VA 22015

Mustang Club
National Capital Region
9397 Shouse Drive
Vienna, VA 22180

Old Dominion Packard Club
901 Dirk Drive
Richmond, VA 23227

VERMONT

Vermont Automobile Enthusiasts
Milton, VT 05468

WASHINGTON

Buick Club of America
Puget Sound Chapter
13003 3rd Ave.
Everett, WA 98204

Cascade V-8 Club
P.O. Box 3811
Federal Way, WA 98063

Early Ford V8 Chapter
Cascade Regional Group
P.O. Box 3811
Federal Way, WA 98003

Ethyl Forever Car Club
P.O. Box 2262
Seattle, WA 98111

Ford-Mercury Club of America
Spokane Chapter
N. 11711 Hemlock St.
Spokane, WA 99218

Henry's Haulers
Ford F100 Truck Club of Western
Washington
1315 Hollis Terrace
Bremerton, WA 98310

Northwest Classic Chevy Club
15010 NE 9th Pl.
Bellevue, WA 98007

Old Dominion Packard Club
Box 533, Fair Street
Bethany, WA 26032

WISCONSIN

Antique Automobile Club of
America
Blackhawk Region
RR3, Rockalve #196
Janesville, WI 53545

Badger State Machines
723 Topeka Dr.
Lake Mills, WI 53551

Buick Club of America
Cream City Chapter
2503 East Whittaker Ave.
St. Francis, WI 53207

Central Wis. Auto Collectors
P.O. Box 2132
Oshkosh, WI 54903

Central Wis. Rods & Customs
P.O. Box 464
Stevens Pt., WI 54481

Classic Car Club of America
Wisconsin Region
9345 N. Waverly Dr.
Bayside, WI 53217

Corsa Chapter
Capital City Corvair Club
4217 Barby Lane
Madison, WI 53704

Fondy Vintage Auto Club
P.O. Box 131
Fond du Lac, WI 54935

Great Lakes Caminos
P.O. Box 13701
Milwaukee, WI 53213

Hudson-Essex-Terraplane
Chicago/Milwaukee Chapter
9059 N. 60th St.
Brown Deer, WI 53223

Mercedes-Benz Club of America
Green Bay Chapter
612 Sunrise Ln.
Green Bay, WI 54301

Milwaukee Corvair Club
2523 E. Armour Av.
Milwaukee, WI 53207

North Central Classics &
    Customs Auto Club
4056 N. Oriole Dr.
Medford, WI 54451

North East Wisconsin Corvair
    Club
1270 Morgan Ave.
Oshkosh, WI 54901

Old Time Auto Club
1507 W. Summer Street
Appleton, WI 54914

Pontiac-Oakland Club
    International
Badger State Chapter
1119 S. 117th St.
West Allis, WI 53214

Pontiac Owners Club
All-American Oakland
120 Mill St.
Iola, WI 54945

River City Street Rods
P.O. Box 434
Eau Claire, WI 54702

Show-N-Go Ltd. Car Club
525 Pine St.
Hartford, WI 53027

Studebaker Drivers Club
Wisconsin Region
217 Farnham St., P.O. Box 772
Marshall, WI 53559

Trans-Am Club of America
Southeast Wisconsin Chapter
P.O. Box 07084
Milwaukee, WI 53207

Waukesha Olde Car Club
P.O. Box 144
Waukesha, WI 53187

Tri-County Antique Auto Club
Rt. 1, Box 39
Unity, WI 54488

48 & Under Car Club
708 Water St.
Sauk City, WI 53583

Wisconsin Edsel Club
1729A S. 24th Street
Milwaukee, WI 53204

Wizards of Rods
5 Madden St.
Mauston, WI 53948

WYOMING

Sweetwater County Street Rods
605 Juniper
Green River, WY 82935

Wyoming Street Rod Association
605 Juniper
Green River, WY 82935

CANADA

Antique & Classic Car Club of
    Canada
12 Clinton Ct.
Brampton, Ontario
L6Z 1Z6 Canada

Classic GTO Club of Ontario
    (Canada)
GTOAA Chapter
149 Victoria Drive
Uxbridge, Ontario
Canada, L0C 1K0

Golden West GTOs (Alberta,
    Canada)
GTOAA Chapter
P.O. Box 403
Midnipore, Alberta
Canada, T0L 1J0

McGlauglin-Buick Club
99 Simcoe St.
Oshawa, Ontario L1H 4G7

Fifty 567 Club
2021 Wiggins Ave.
Saskatoon, Sask. S7J 1W2

Golden West (Canada)
GTO Association of America
    Chapter
Box 403
Midnipore Post Office
Calgary, Alberta T0L 1J0

Rolls-Royce Owners Club
British Columbia Region
2586 Lawson Ave.
West Vancouver, BC
Canada V7V 2E9

Citroenian
49 Mungo Park Way
Orpington, Kent BR5 4EE
England

Citronews
P.O. Box 43
Walkerville, South Africa

Auto Credits

1941 *Hudson*   Mike Gajdek/NJ

1948 *Tucker*   Jack Bart/NY

1948 *Oldsmobile*   Steve Aprigliano/NY

1949 *Buick*   John Harrington/NJ

1949 *Kaiser*   Fred Kanter/NJ

1949 *Packard*   Alan Glucksman/NJ

1950 *Pontiac*   Charles Januska/NY

1950 *Mercury Coupe*   James Ragsdale/NJ

1951 *Nash*   Dan Kanter/NJ

1952 *Packard*   Fred Kanter/NJ

1953 *Buick Skylark*   Richard Allocca/NJ

1953 *Oldsmobile 88 Convertible*   Jeff Griggs/NJ

1953 *Kaiser Manhattan*   John Harrington/NJ

1954 *Lincolns*   James Ragsdale/NJ

1954 *Cadillac Fleetwood*   Steve Aprigliano/NY

1954 *Mercury Sun Valley*   Patrick Antonacci/NY

1954 *Studebaker*   Sue Gala & Tom Tirado/NY

1955 *Chevrolet Bel Air*   Edward Sparacio/NY

1955 *Mercury*   El Viajero/NY

1955 *Packard Caribbean*   Dan Kanter/NJ

1956 *Chevrolet Bel Air*   Richard Allocca/NJ

1956 *Packard 400 (two)*   William Le Gall/NJ

1956 *Oldsmobile 88 Hardtop*   Manuel Ruiz/NY

1956 *Imperial*   N.Y.C. parade car

1957 *Chevrolet Bel Air*   Steven Martindale/NJ

1957 *Pontiac Safari*   Patrick Magee/NY

1957 *Dodge*   Michael & Roseann Talbot/NJ

1957 *T-Bird*   (Mustard color) James Ragsdale/NJ

1957 *Lincoln Continental Mark II*   James Ragsdale/NJ

1955 *T-Bird (red)*   Sonny Cestaro/NJ

1956 *T-Bird (white)*   Sonny Cestaro/NJ

1957 *T-Bird (blue)*   Sonny Cestaro/NJ

1950 *Mercury (Leadsled)*   Joel T. Sheipe/NY

1957 *Oldsmobile (Precious & Few)*   Joel T. Sheipe/NY

1958 *Cadillac Eldorado Convertible*   Dave Barclay/NJ

1958 *Cadillac Eldorado Brougham*   Dave Barclay/NJ

1958 *Cadillac Sedan de Ville*   Jay Hirsch/NY

1958 *DeSoto*   Donald Piscitelli/NJ

1958 *Pontiac Bonneville*   Bill Harrington/NJ

1959 *Edsel*   Stewart Siegel/NY

1959 *Ford Skyliner*   Donald Wilenkin/CA

1959 *Cadillac Limousine*   Dave Brega/NY

1959 *Cadillac Fleetwood 60*   Marvin Hirsch/NY

1959 *Oldsmobile 98*   Fitzroy Gittens/NY

1960 *Nash Metropolitan*   John Harrington/NJ

1960 *Nash Rambler*   Mike Gajdek/NJ

1960 *Imperial*   Donald Piscitelli/NJ

1960 *Cadillac Fleetwood 60*   Sarah Hirsch/NY

1960 *Plymouth Fury Convertible*   Sue Cooney/NJ

1960 *T-Bird*   Buddy Braun/NJ

1962 *T-Bird*   Jack Bart/NY

1962 *Cadillac Fleetwood*   Frank Leogrande/NY

1963 *Ghia*   Fred Kanter/NJ

1963 *Lincoln Continental*   Jay Hirsch/NY

1963 *Pontiac Tempest Convertible*   Jay Hirsch/NY

1963 *Studebaker Avanti*   Lester Waller/NY

1964 *Cadillac Fleetwood*   Terry Talley/NY

1965 *AMC/Marlin*   Mike Gajdek/NJ

1965 *Studebaker Daytona*   Donald Cook/NJ

1966 *Mustang (Coupe, Convertible)*   Dan Brautman/NY

1966 *Mustang (Fastback)*   Frank A. Bonanno Jr./NY

1967 *Camaro SS Convertible*   Marty Dunn/NY

1968 **AMC/AMX**   Lester Waller/NY
1969 *Camaro* Z-28   James Parseghian/NJ
1970 *Pontiac* G.T.O.   Dominick Leogrande/
NY
1973 *Cadillac Eldorado Convertible*   Marvin
Hirsch/NY

Index